ROSES AND GLADIOLI by Fantin-Latour
This Book Belongs to—
Geneva Jordan
Jan - 1963

D1058388

HARVEST OF HOPE

BOOKS BY FAITH BALDWIN

Three Women
Departing Wings
Alimony
The Office-Wife
The Incredible Year
Make-Believe
Today's Virtue
Skyscraper
Week-end Marriage
District Nurse
Self-made Woman
Beauty
White-Collar Girl
Love's a Puzzle
Innocent Bystander
Wife versus Secretary
Within a Year
Honor Bound
American Family
The Puritan Strain
The Moon's Our Home
Private Duty
The Girls of Divine Corners
Men Are Such Fools!
That Man Is Mine
The Heart Has Wings
Twenty-four Hours a Day
Manhattan Nights
Enchanted Oasis
Rich Girl, Poor Girl
Hotel Hostess
The High Road
Career by Proxy
White Magic
Station Wagon Set
Rehearsal for Love
"Something Special"
Letty and the Law
Medical Center
And New Stars Burn
Temporary Address: Reno
The Heart Remembers
Blue Horizons
Breath of Life
Five Women in Three Novels
The Rest of My Life with You
Washington, U.S.A.
You Can't Escape
He Married a Doctor
Change of Heart
Arizona Star
A Job for Jenny
No Private Heaven
Woman on Her Way
Sleeping Beauty
Give Love the Air
Marry for Money
They Who Love
The Golden Shoestring
Look Out for Liza
The Whole Armor
The Juniper Tree
Face Toward the Spring
Three Faces of Love
Many Windows
Blaze of Sunlight
Testament of Trust
The West Wind
Harvest of Hope

POETRY

Sign Posts
Widow's Walk

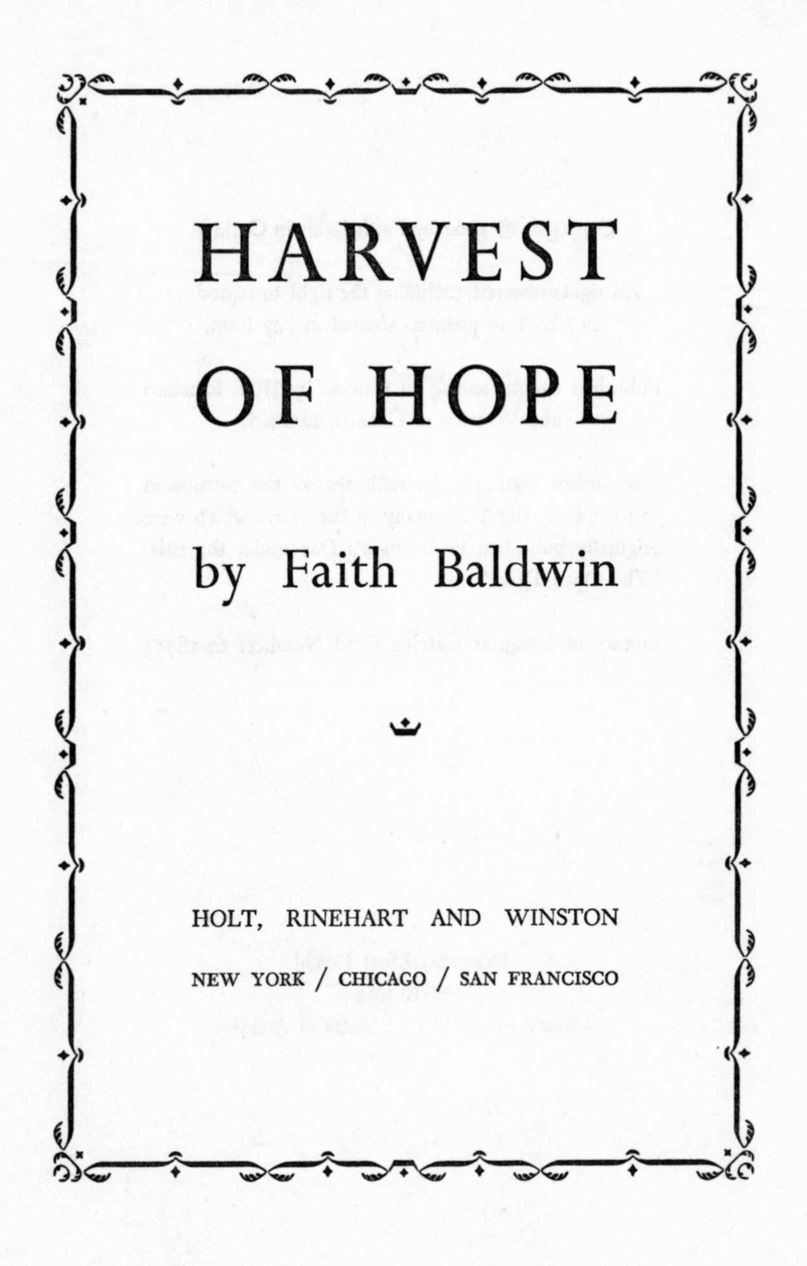

HARVEST OF HOPE

by Faith Baldwin

HOLT, RINEHART AND WINSTON
NEW YORK / CHICAGO / SAN FRANCISCO

Published simultaneously in Canada by Holt, Rinehart
and Winston of Canada, Limited.

The author acknowledges with thanks the permission to include in this book many of the essays which were originally published in *Woman's Day* under the title, "The Open Door."

Library of Congress Catalog Card Number: 62-18753

Designer: Ernst Reichl
80793-1012
Printed in the United States of America

For my sister, my children,

and friends,

and all whom they love.

FOREWORD

♛

IT IS entirely true that what we sow, we reap. Sow love and trust and joy, and when the crops are garnered, this is what you will have. Sow their opposites and these you will glean. I am aware that this is, nowadays, called the unrealistic or the wishful-thinking approach; it used to be called a Pollyanna attitude. But I am not disturbed. I permit other people to think as they will, and ask for myself only the same privilege.

In my belief, a harvest is also a legacy, for very often what you reap is, in the way of small miracles, more than you consciously know you have sown. And in my stubborn conviction, a legacy need not be of material substance or —in the usual employment of the term—bestowed after an owner no longer has use for it. To consider a harvest or an inheritance valid only if you can hold it in your hands, deposit it in the bank, display it in your living room, or sell it in the open market, is merely the letter of the law. That which a man gives to life and takes or derives from life is his harvest and his legacy for all his mortal years; that of himself which during those years he gives to others, undiluted, is theirs—a harvest for them and, in effect, a living trust.

Every moment of every hour brings harvest and has a gift to offer. I have, therefore, rewrapped some of my own for you.

A few of these came not in the shapes of joy but of sorrow, yet after one has lived with them for a while they seem to be textbooks from which a lesson is to be learned.

It has increasingly become the fashion to travel—abroad or in one's own country, so will you come with me on, say, a thirteen-month trip—as sidereal time is calculated—and experience some of the large and small events, the land- and sea-scapes, the side tours, which constitute a little span of living?

Now, begin with me, if you will, in the month of December, a very giving time.

HARVEST OF HOPE

DECEMBER

Early in this month I begin to put away the everyday things and bring from the attic the bits and pieces, the music boxes and angels, which give the house the Christmas look. I also take out my seasonal apron; it is impractical but pretty—sequin-embroidered with trees and holly berries.

One thing I shall not find in the attic is what is called the Christmas spirit. No carton can hold this, only the human heart . . . and this spirit is always universal and not confined to creed. At this time of year those of the Jewish faith celebrate the Festival of Lights, Hanukah, and for eight days the Menorah stands in many windows, holding the lighted candles. This is also a time of gifts.

All creeds, the world around, have their special celebrations of giving, gratitude, and acknowledgment.

The living holly which I can see from the south window has steadily grown in height and girth these past ten years and bears a multitude of berries. I remember my delight when, in 1939, I saw streets in Canberra, Australia, lined with English holly trees. I had just one holly tree at home, and by the time I moved to where I now live, it was very big. I hated to leave it, but, oh, how the one at the new home has grown! Very soon, the birds will strip it of berries, but for a while I can look out and see bare ground or dazzling snow, according to the weather, and the fruit shining among the dark green leaves.

The birds' Christmas tree is something of a problem. It grows near the little terrace and has become very tall, and a step ladder is not practical for me—I am too unsteady on my feet—although I do risk using a small one when trimming my indoor tree, hanging onto the bookshelves with one hand. Well, the birds will just have to lower themselves. After all, what are wings for unless to fly low as well as high? This year I think I'll try doughnuts tied with red ribbon, popcorn strings, and lots of suet.

There is a certain tranquility in the simple act of feeding birds—even those you'd rather not; the starlings, for instance—in sitting by a big window in any season to watch them come to the feeders, in brilliant plumage or dull. Tranquility, if we allow ourselves to become aware of it, can be a special gift of Christmastime, even during the multiple activities. But in any season of the year we should consciously seek tranquility within ourselves, for the uncertainty and tension under which our world now lives seem to have communicated themselves even to this period, the keynote of which should be peace.

Many of my friends have become either extremely cautious or wildly extravagant in planning their gifts and festivities. It seems to me that in this, as in everything else, the middle way is best. Still, I do firmly believe in the occasional extravagance. Remember the women you know who, when they are utterly depressed, go forth and buy hats they can't afford? I've never had depression affect me after this manner though once, leaving a luncheon at which I'd been a speaker, I did stop and buy a piece of millinery far beyond my means. My only excuse was that I felt very queer. Indeed, I should have; my temperature was 104!

My extravagances are usually—not always—for someone else. I do not buy people hats. What woman in her right mind would buy a hat for another woman? I pause here to comment that I know one who did. She bought it for me. It is very becoming, thank you, and I wear it with pleasure. But I do not trust my taste in hats for anyone else.

Last summer—as in other summers—I bought Christmas presents. My sister, whom I visit each June, poor girl, lives near Home, Sweet Home where the writer of that immortal song once lived. It is now a charming museum and I brought back from it a clutch of tea tiles. What could be more appropriate than to give someone Home, Sweet Home for Christmas?

In August, I went antiquing and found special things for special people. Next week, I'm going to have to go up to the storeroom to look for them, for I have a wretched trick of putting such carefully selected gifts away and then forgetting where.

Each October, I go to a nearby shop which has an imaginative owner-buyer and replenish the tree or house ornaments. I have lost a couple of angels from old age. Of course real angels never age, but mine being mere representations just quietly fell apart, though I was happy to discover last night that the table decorations are intact. When I remember that the centerpiece is over thirty years old, it astonishes me. It looks far less weathered than I, but then, I'm thirty years old twice over and have not been put in the attic to rest for eleven months of each year.

I was in a bookshop last fall, looking—naturally—at books and choosing some to send to friends in Australia and New Zealand, and for others in Holland and England. The owner of the shop has suffered with me before and knows that the Down Under books must be sent in October if they are to reach the Antipodes by the time their very warm, sunny, summer Christmas comes. While we were discussing this and that, a woman I know came in and asked me why I was buying books on New England and books of cartoons. When I answered, "For Christmas," she said, dramatically, that she couldn't bear it, not only the foresight but the fact that I was troubling about Christmas at all when the world might blow up at any time.

I conceded that it might, though I seriously doubted it, and even if I didn't, it wasn't a valid reason for me to sit and wait, shaking, at home, with the shades down, the birds unfed, no packages wrapped and ready, and no angels to fly from doorways and mantelpieces.

A friend wrote me a while ago, saying, "Isn't it wonderful that the future comes just one day at a time?" That is a good thing to think about. She's right, you know. Even the most careful, long-range planning can be upset in a space as short as a clock's tick. And as long as the future does come one day at a time, surely we were meant to live that day as fully and normally as possible? And I'm glad that every day of this month brings the Eve twenty-four hours nearer.

I realize the gravity of the world situation, but I am not going to be cheated by it of my one-day-at-a-time. I am going to look for, and find, tranquility under the Christmas tree, in the stocking hanging at the fireplace, and within my heart and spirit.

Few of us still celebrate this season where first we learned its meaning. How many rooms, apartments, or houses has each of us decorated in the course of our lives so far? In recent years the families of servicemen have found themselves following the Christmas tradition in many lands which, not long since, were just names on maps to them. My own Christmas days have been spent in a number of houses and apartments—my parents', my own, and the homes of friends, in the North, in the East, and in the subtropics—and I've looked out to snow or its absence, to pine trees or palms.

Nowadays young people move with breath-taking rapidity. So many junior executives, for instance, are transferred almost at the moment they've bought houses and settled down. The wife of one wrote me that, in seven years of marriage, she'd moved five times and had not been able to make friends. Oh, but she could have, even during a short time in one place or another.

This is the season when many families gather together and read aloud the Christmas story. Whatever our creed may be, three words hold promise and hope for us all, and these are, "Peace on Earth." I know it appears impossible to attain, yet somehow I don't think it is. We are told by the historians that the world can never escape wars, but it should be everyone's goal to work toward the fulfillment of the ancient promise. And if one asks: "But what can I do?", I suppose there is one answer which has nothing to do with organizations, diplomacy, treaties, politics, or preachments, and that is to try to establish peace in our own hearts and minds and surroundings. If everyone would, you know, they'd prove the historians wrong. I believe firmly that whatever path a man travels in his journey toward his Creator, he will find upon it the quiet turning asides, the resting places provided for thanksgiving, trust, and sharing.

This Christmas, whether it snows or not, will be different

from all the others. In our family, as in so many others, long months of war once left empty chairs at the dinner table; and children were absent on many occasions during their growing up and later in homes of their own. But last year, when a visiting daughter and I were trimming the tree, word came that one of us would never come home again for a brief holiday, would never again speak to us over the distance, by telephone, during the season. So Christmas becomes different and, for his brother and sisters, for his mother and his wife, and for his little uncomprehending children, difficult.

Yet, in Christmas, which is birth and joy, there is the promise of Easter, which is rebirth and joy, and at another time, there is Thanksgiving. . . .

Gratitude is a humble emotion. It expresses itself in a thousand ways, from a sincere thank you to friend or stranger, to the mute, upreaching acknowledgment to God—not for the gifts of this day only, but for the day itself; not for what we believe will be ours in the future, but for the bounty of the past.

Last year, in this house, we finished trimming the tree, and this year it will also be trimmed. I have believed for many years that those who have loved us continue to do so, and loving us, still share. The wound of absence remains; but the believing in the continuity of life and love is balm.

The key word, the touchstone, is "love," and basically Christmas is just that.

For a long time I deplored the tension, the rushing about, and what is known as the commercialism of this season, but in the last few years I have learned to ignore these aspects, for, after all, the bright wrapping is not the gift itself; you can discard the tissue paper and the holly-imprinted box and look within it and know that someone thought of you.

Every December, a string of old sleigh bells, set on cracking leather, hangs outside our door. Weather-beaten by wind, snow, ice, and rain, the sturdy leather has survived, and when you shake the string of bells, their tone remains true and clear.

Our indoor tree—on its green felt cloth, and a new red one, which has my name embroidered on it by friends—does not stand in its special corner for more than a week or ten days because the needles fall. So, after a while, the ornaments are removed and put in their labeled boxes and the tree is taken outside and burned. Somewhat later the outdoor wreaths, denuded of their scarlet bows, are put out in the fields, with cones and berries still intact for the birds to enjoy. But these are only symbols and in discarding them, as sooner or later we must, we need not, if gratitude is in us, discard, in the months to come, the remembrance of all the holiday has meant to us and will mean again.

Do not take Christmas up to the attic and put it away with the cartons of ornaments. Keep it with you all year long—the out-goingness, the giving, the loving impulse.

"What can I give," folks sometimes ask me, "to someone who has everything?"

I don't suppose anyone really has everything. Oh, there are people who can afford all the material things they want, but *everything* is rather a large order. And anyone can give love and understanding, no matter what else. You can't wrap these in crimson or silver, gold or green; you can't tie them with ribbons; you can't mail them, unless in a letter or card. But love and understanding are gifts which endure from December to December; they cannot be tarnished, nor will moths invade them; they cannot fade, or be destroyed, or stolen. And nothing you can buy in any shop in the world can ever match them in beauty and value.

Always at this season we are able to extend ourselves a little . . . if we make it a lot, it will stretch from Christmas to Christmas. That's my Christmas vow.

What can I give you but this, and the belief that we share—you with me and I with you—each other's way of celebrating? December twenty-fifth comes to us during our northern winter and, a few days before, we experience the shortest day of the year. Then the days begin imperceptibly to lengthen, and by February we recognize the added moments of light. More light, always more light, and a turning toward spring, while on the other side of the Equator it is already summer.

Climates differ, people differ, and we live in a rapidly altering world. Try to take a little time from the inevitable increasing pressures and the anxieties, to share with others those things which are forever lasting—courage, hope, love.

And have a blessed, happy Christmas wherever you may be.

I, December, being of sound mind . . .

Each month leaves us an inheritance. In this part of the world, jewels are lavishly bestowed. Snow, falling like pearls from the pewter casket of the sky; berries which are ruby and garnet; the various greens of pine and spruce and cedar —dark jade, spinach jade, emerald, peridot. And when ice has formed on branch and bough and the sun shines again, we look upon a world of diamonds. The snow, new-fallen, is ermine on the ground and trees. And when it melts, and we see the tall dried grasses of the field, there's a strange topaz light which shines through them.

December leaves us its legacy of events; we remember carols and singing children and the Christmas warmth. Those of us who have fireplaces have watched the brilliant, secret life of the flames and the gem-bright embers burning away.

December has brought joy to many, and to some sorrow. Every month leaves one or the other, or both, with us. In some houses there is mourning, and in some rejoicing; a man dies, a child is born. But the harvest of hope remains.

The book you happened to read, which made so great an impression on you; a friend you had not seen in many years stopping by; a letter from one you have known since you were a child; new friends, growing dear, even in the first meeting; the telephone call you did not expect . . . did December leave you any of these to remember it by?

Whatever else December has given us, it certainly gave work and play, responsibility and that weightless added measure of maturity which each month leaves behind it.

So, thank you, December.

JANUARY

Don't look now, but I think I hear the new year stirring around the house. I hope it has brought with it a new broom with which to sweep out old debris—disappointments, discouragements, folly.

However, I don't often think of a new year as a housemaid, but as one who brings us a sort of Pandora's box. We aren't forbidden to open it, of course; it's just that we can't; it will open by itself in time, and there will be many things inside: the good, the bad, and the indifferent. We all know what to expect—principally, the totally unexpected.

Quite a number of new years have come into the houses where I have lived. I've been sitting here quietly thinking about them and the changes they've brought to me, and to everyone of my age.

How about this year? I wonder.

We all wonder. . . . For a long time we have felt the knife-edge of uncertainty, cold and sharp, and feeling it, have pondered possible alterations in our ways of living. We have thought of things we don't want to think about.

Yet, when we stop to consider it, this is not a new attitude. Every year brings uncertainty, the inability to look very far ahead, and, of course, inevitable changes. Not all of these are part of the larger world, the universal problems; many are related only to our individual selves and ways of life.

Whether or not it's justified, I think each of us has a touching faith in a new year. It's like the new broom I spoke of, or a new house, a new job—a new anything. Leave the old, we think; sweep it out; bring in the new; it's bound to be better! There is something intensely personal in the air for each of us when the clock strikes midnight. And in the short space of its striking, one year is gone and another begun. Somehow, in anything new, there is always a core of hope.

For goodness knows how many years artists have been depicting the old year as a tottering ancient and the new as a baby. I suppose it's the conventional way to do it, but I never saw a one-year-old child sporting a long white beard and leaning on a cane; as for the new year's baby, it actually comes to us rather older than it looks in the drawings, for it has a considerable heritage of time and history.

One's birthday is a special kind of new year. To be sure, we share our birthdays with thousands of other people, but not everyone who celebrates when we do was born in the same year, place, hour, and minute—surely there's a little we can claim for our very own. But the crossing from one year to the next, in the sense of sidereal time, in the tick of a watch, is something we do share with everyone, even though the Iranians, Russians, and Chinese celebrate on other dates.

It has taken me a long time to learn that the answers to the problems of change lie in ourselves. I can't begin to tell you the struggle it has been to a person as organized as I, with—in most situations—an orderly mind, to adjust to sudden alterations. I wasn't born that way; I had to achieve it. The trick I've learned—and you *can* teach an old dog new tricks—is to go right ahead and make plans and then, if things change, cancel them. Some people are born adaptable, but some, like myself, have to learn the hard way.

I'm not especially flexible with myself, either. I don't know anyone who irritates me more than myself. I am, as I have said, an essentially tidy creature, and also a small one, incredibly clumsy or absent-minded, or both. I stub toes; I whack fingers; I close windows on my hands—these old windows fall down with the greatest of ease and a loud crash of triumph. Every day of my life I mislay or lose something and go around like the White Rabbit, muttering, "Oh, dear; oh, dear," and feeling terribly sorry for myself. I burn myself on stoves. I also burn the toast. Not long ago I scorched the cupboards above the toaster. I scald myself with hot water. . . . Why, oh why, did I mention water? I'm always spilling it. I no sooner arrange flowers to my satisfaction and start to carry them someplace else than I am forced to set them down and run for a cloth or mop. So I expect to go forward into this year, dropping and losing things.

I no sooner put an address carefully aside than it gets up and walks, all by itself, into the wastebasket. When that happens, someone immediately empties the small wastebasket into the bigger one on the back porch and I have to go out and rustle through it. I did that only this morning and it was perishing cold outside. I expect to forget my keys when I go out at night; I expect to bark my shins and bang my knees. I am not calling all this down upon myself, mind you; I am just deciding to be prepared, and I am making one small pledge, which is, not to get as mad at me as I usually do.

Last summer I returned home from a happy evening at the theater. It was quite late, since we'd stopped for coffee afterward, and when I came in, I rushed upstairs and opened a lot of windows because the night was very hot. I had just turned on the window-fan in my bedroom when the skies began to roll with thunder. I turned off the fan, closed the windows again, and in a very few minutes I was alone in one of the worst storms I've ever experienced. After one particularly bright flash, my two bedside lights went out. I found a flashlight and, shaking, prowled through the house. Not until I chanced to look at an electric clock did it occur to me to try the other lights. . . . They were all working.

I notice that other people suffer from the same defects as I, but their shortcomings don't irritate me.

There's a lesson in all this: When something unexpected and terrifying happens in this new year, and the nearby lights go out—try the others. There are so many lights we forget to try, though the switches are handy; one is that of turning quietly to the Light of the World, which is God. The darkness in the little room of the personal self is real enough, but beyond it, there is light.

You often hear people speak of the "moment of truth." Books have been written around that title; you encounter the words in fiction and in nonfiction. But there are many moments of truth in a year's time.

Truth is a key which unlocks many doors; it can also be a door which many keys can open. Yet I mostly think of it as a bridge—from moment to moment, hour to hour; a bridge between weeks, months and years; and from one life to the next. We must never be afraid to cross the bridges.

JANUARY

This being January, I am resigned to snow. If I am indoors, I love to watch it fall, with its own white silence. Outdoors, in the fields and woods, I like to walk through it, provided I am properly dressed. I do not enjoy it under the wheels of a car or obscuring a windshield. Sometimes, when there's little or no snow in this month, February comes roaring in like a white whirlwind.

Snow or no snow, I hope the starlings, which have plagued me for so long, decide that another climate is better. I haven't much hope, for they greatly enjoy the bird seed.

A few doves will winter here and perhaps my lone towhee. The cardinals and the blue jays will come in numbers; so will my regular visitors, nuthatches and woodpeckers, sparrows and juncos and chickadees. And the pheasant will tiptoe delicately over the snow or the brown earth.

I shall—heaven help me!—be working on a book begun some time ago, and suffering, therefore, the usual frustrations, pangs, dissatisfactions, and anxieties. No matter how many books you write, the next one is always the hardest. But I like to work in the winter, wrapped in the silence of the snow and the awareness of clear frosty air outside, or even when the north wind screams down the chimneys and rattles the doors and windows. For the house is warm, and there are always flowers in it, and now and then the telephone rings and someone asks, "How are you?"

There's a stillness in winter which cannot be found at any other season. In summer, the windows stand wide, cars whoosh past, dogs race about the fields, hay is cut, and the neighbors have frequent cookouts, usually accompanied by long-playing records. In spring, everything seems to stir —you can practically hear the plants growing—and people are out cleaning up their yards. Boys play ball in the road, the bicycles go by. In autumn the parade of cars is as ceaseless as in summer—the stream of city or country folk out looking at the foliage. And the sounds of building, the whine of power saws, seem to pervade all seasons except winter.

These are the nights of the dinner-plate stars, the silver service of celestial banquets, polished to an incredible brilliance, and the curious sensation that your own world within the world is enclosed in a crystal cave. Winter is, I think, a good time for the working writer. There are far too many distractions outdoors in the other seasons. I'm always leaving a half-finished sentence to tear outside, observe a bird, cut a flower, or pull a weed; or I go out to stand close to a lilac bush and breathe the fragrance, to look under a mat of fallen leaves for the first violet, or to walk along the scarlet paths of autumn. I am not, however, athletic by nature, and skis have no appeal. I could never learn to skate, and my sledding days are very far behind me. Now and then, on a clear, sunny winter day, I will, as I've said, walk in a field, stepping gingerly along in snow boots, and I'll even go out occasionally to clear the bird feeders of ice and snow. But usually I depart from the house only when I must—to go to church, or to the hairdresser, to a speaking or dinner engagement, or to a party.

As always, I make no resolutions when the new year comes. I'd never keep them, so why a one-day determination, just because the last numeral on the year's figure changes? I usually make a vow or two to myself. But I believe that this year, instead of making a vow, I'll ask for a gift. I'll ask for direction, guidance, and help. I need to be more patient, to grow in comprehension, to learn to take things as they come, to be less annoyed with myself, and to find a cure for the chronic worry, which now and again erupts to the surface.

There are a great many things I'd like to complete in this year. The most I can do is try. There are also things I want to do. I'd like so much to indulge myself, for instance, with a long trip—to some familiar spot, London, for choice; or to somewhere new to me. But as the year begins, I do not see my way clear. One of the best lessons we can learn, I suppose, is to seek the fulfillment of a dream, but if it does not come true, to dismiss it—until the next time. After all, we've had the pleasure of dreaming. No one attains all he desires and no one realizes all his dreams. It's better so. If we had everything right now, what would be left to wish for and where would the future lead? I suppose on a straight line instead of turning corners. Yet turning corners is half of living. We don't know what's around the bend and I doubt if we're supposed to know.

In January, many people get into a great state, moaning about the long winter ahead. But with every day that passes, winter becomes shorter. So, together with my house, I'll just settle down to it, knowing that what will be, will be. I am not a fatalist—I believe we make our own happiness or unhappiness as we obey or disobey physical and spiritual laws—but there are also events beyond our conscious control.

I have lived through a good many things which were unrelated to my thinking or determination . . . illnesses of those I love, the final termination of which I guessed, and so was rebellious. And also through a stunning bolt from the blue which I had never once considered.

These things we must learn to take in our spiritual stride, however unhappy we are, although resigning ourselves to what we call God's will seems a little spineless to me. To *accept* God's will is something else again—resignation and acceptance being two different attitudes of mind.

Every year presents its problems, also its opportunities;

every year affords a challenge. With the uneasiness now affecting our small planet, perhaps the best thing we can do is to welcome both opportunity and challenge, meet the problems, face the realities, and not add to the vast sum of human unhappiness by revealing our tensions, which always spread from us to family and friends and eventually affect everyone we meet and even those we never meet.

This year, I'll ask, in all humility, for a measure of inner and outer tranquility. I'll ask also for strength to trust and, therefore, to put the next twelve months into God's strong, quiet hands.

For you, I wish a Happy New Year. I don't wish for you everything you want, for there must always be something ahead to desire. But I do wish for you, with all my heart, rewards and pleasant astonishments, and always the ability to adjust, the willingness to be—or to become—flexible, and for that Light upon your path which no personal darkness can ever quench.

There is always a new year. If you don't feel like celebrating right now, wait until the Chinese make a festival of theirs. . . . Or what about Iran? I can't get used to the new name of this beautiful country I've longed to see, and never have seen. I still think of it as Persia. I dream of Persian gardens and of a collection of Persian miniatures. . . . Well, Iran celebrates the new year on the very first day of spring. Think of that, and remember that a new year —whatever the calendar date—is still a beginning.

So to you and the world, a Happy New Year.

I, January . . .

The old year having been harvested, the new year is sown —yet, in actuality, it was sown an eternity ago. And the legacy of January, this first month, is the imperceptible lengthening of the days, the added minutes of sunlight, and a reaching ahead. And in the present second, long blue shadows on the snow and the sparkle of sunshine upon treacherous ice—for there are two sides to everything—in this case, beauty and danger.

The harvest of each year is implicit in January, the gift of the unknown months and the path ahead.

To me, January gives with generous hands: so often the stormy white world outside the windows; and indoors, warmth and comfort and pleasure in growing things. I do not have a green thumb and I agonize over my African violets—for my sister and many of my friends they grow lavishly—and over the coleus, the one with the pink and green leaves; and the begonia, with its tight miniature-rose blossoms, called by its giver, a Hungarian bleeding heart.

January affords me such strong, hot sunlight at the

south windows—even when the outdoor-terrace thermometer reads zero—that I can't sit for long in the brilliant rays. It gives me time to think and work and requires that my timid physical body venture forth on snow and ice to keep an engagement, see a friend, or meet an obligation.

January leaves me—leaves all of us—the reminder that the year is new. Its bequest is upreaching hope, a will to nurture courage, a going forward, and the promise of golden, enduring harvest in the future. It gives us opportunity—as do all the months of all the years.

So, thank you, January.

FEBRUARY

Fᴇʙʀᴜᴀʀʏ, in this neck of the woods, is the month when I look at my engagement calendar and wonder if invited guests can make it over the snow and ice to dinner . . . and, even more importantly, if Gussie, who cooks for me, will get here from her home, some miles distant? Whoever comes may have to totter in, stamping the snow from their overshoes and hastily closing the door . . . or, if it isn't snow they close it against, perhaps a slash of rain, a gust of wind. It is also the month when, if I have to go out, I wonder, for several days ahead, if I can.

A month of moods, a halting place between winter and spring, a "waiting month" as a friend wrote me recently —a creeping out of or into storms. Usually, a miserable month, that can set you back on your heels, and rock you right off them if there's ice beneath. Still, we go forward.

A year ago my older daughter was married on the morn of what proved to be our worst and most crippling blizzard, which came with a sudden violence after bride and groom had reached the city for a weekend wedding trip. Cars were unable to move after the storm struck, so there they were, walking in the snow, in an empty town, a city of silence. But if love laughs at locksmiths, it also laughs at blizzards.

This is the month of that timid soul, the ground hog. I do not believe in him as a prophet because there just have to be places where he sees his shadow and others where he doesn't. I suppose the persistent ground-hog addicts would say that winter remains in the one section and departs in the other. Very well, I'll concede that, and I suppose I'll have to bow to the cricket also: six weeks to frost when you hear the first cricket. The catch here is: how do you know he's the first? Maybe you weren't listening the night or the week before. . . . And, by the way, I don't believe in "woolly bears" either!

There's one thing in which I do believe and that's the bell-like sound of the peepers, speaking from their comfortable mud in the silence of the night. When I hear the first ones, I know it's spring. Still, I'm told that they have to be frozen back—is it three times?—before the prediction comes true. The farther south you go, the sooner you hear them.

Country folks tell me that the first skunk you encounter on the road—usually run over, poor animal—is also a sure sign of spring's arrival. I think, too, of red-winged black birds; occasionally they come at the end of this month, with that clear unmistakable call to lift the wintry heart. And early this month someone reported a skunk cabbage in the woods, but perhaps it was just precocious.

I don't set my year's clock by the robin any more, for robins have taken to wintering over with us. When I look out and there's a flock of them sailing in, then I'm sure it's spring, but not when I see a loner, wondering what on earth has happened to the worms?

Daytime gales and blowing storms and bitter chill, l
when it's clear, the wonderful nights.

Each month we experience the dark of the moon whi
affected primitive races (and even some not so primitiv
with superstitious awe. There are moon-rules which st
seem credible to many people, and perhaps they're righ
There are the planting times, for instance, and the som
what lesser regulations governing the cutting of one's nail
and hair. And you mustn't start a new venture when th
moon is waning! Unfortunately, perhaps, that's a rul
few of us can afford to obey.

When no moon is visible to the human eye, the night's darkness seems denser—except, of course, when stars shine through—but it's comforting to know that the moon is still there. Nature has not removed it from the cradle of the sky and put it away for a little while. Soon there will be a silver sliver, then the growing, horned crescent, and finally the full noble light. When this month's full moon floods down, the unearthly illumination on snow and ice, or on bare boughs which look as if they were silver-plated, will take one's breath. And if a branch is weighted with snow, you look upon white blossoming.

We, who are children of the earth—operating under Divine Will and natural laws, physical and spiritual—have our own moon phases, all through the year—darkness, delivery from darkness, the waning, the waxing, and again the waning. None lives, except the mindless, who do not, in some degree experience this—hours of despair, followed by the brightening hope; or slow adjustment, moments of fear, even panic, and then, the light, however small. For the normal human being it would be impossible to live every hour of every day under emotional stress; there must be, on this seesaw of living, periods of even balance.

This month is our shortest. To be sure it isn't shortened

much, but twenty-eight days are less than thirty or thirty-one, even in my arithmetic. So we are closer to next month —which means that the bills arrive earlier.

It is hard for me to divide anything by anything, except two, so I always have difficulty in determining Leap Year. I could look in the almanac, but I rely, instead, on my Leap Year birthday friends, or the newspapers, to remind me. I doubt if girls nowadays take advantage of Leap Year, in the old-time sense. But history tells us that once many asked men they knew would not accept to marry them in order to stock up on silk dresses—the forfeit for refusal.

This is the month of celebrated birthdays. I have a close friend, the pastor of my church, whose birthday falls between Lincoln's and Washington's. Vainly, I endeavor to convince him that he must be unusual, for the astrologers say that Aquarius, the sign under which he was born, produces more geniuses than any other. But he does not believe me.

This is also the month of Saint Valentine. I am devoted to him because he permits me to send all the valentines the budget will permit and, with nine grandchildren, I have to buy hearts and flowers in bulk. Then there are my sister, her husband, the parents of the grandchildren, a great many friends, and one valentine birthday. I buy my cards as early as possible and address them; of course, I mislay some; and somehow I never have enough. In the last few years, I've been happy to see that the pretty ones are back in favor, those which look rather like the valentines of my youth—doves and roses, lattice windows, paper lace.

I have some old ones; a framed one was sent to me by a daughter-in-law; two which came recently are on the library bookshelf. Another was sent to me by a reader who has a

great collection of antique valentines; her gift, she said, might remind me of my youth, dating as it did from the 1880's. That hurt my vanity, as did the remark of another friend when I wrote that I had spoken at a meeting of the blizzard boys and girls of 1888, and he replied he was astonished that I remembered. Well, I don't! I was just at the meeting to repeat what my mother had told me!

But to return to valentines . . . I've never grown out of being a romanticist and a sentimentalist and I'm not sorry in the least.

People who cannot observe the little celebrations, traditions, holidays, and customs with a lifting of their hearts are not, I think, basically happy. To be bored by all this, to see only commercial aspects and to lack enthusiasm for the little celebrations, even if it denotes a childlike attitude, is to have missed one of the really great gifts. The sense of adventure, the upsurge of affection which should be expressed, and the sheer delight which is, in essence, of the spirit, are perhaps the only things we carry over from childhood, except the somewhat dubious ones of heredity and remembered environment.

The happiest people I know haven't much, materially—I do not mean that they live in grinding poverty and constant terror; those who do are not happy, of course; no one is, under fear—I mean that they have enough to eat, roofs over their heads, clothes against the cold and, though budgets have to be stretched, they possess a hundred enthusiasms which means twice, five times, a hundred friends.

These are the people who give their hands and their hearts. They can't run out to the florist, the specialty shop, the jeweler, the car dealer, or the dress shop, and say, "Charge it, please." They don't say, "Charge it," at all. They say, "I made this for you," or, "I thought of you when

I looked at this today. It was my mother's; I'm sure she'd like you to have it." They find books in out-of-print shops, and small treasures in secondhand stores; they grow plants or herbs in pots and put them on your window sills; they send newspaper items which will interest you; they knit, crochet, tat, and sew; they do a little Sunday painting; they bake cookies and cakes for you, or cranberry bread; and they never forget you when they put up pickles and preserves for their own families. What are they giving you? They are giving themselves.

How fortunate I have been in having known so many generous people! Many who can afford the material gift gave it so freely and lovingly that part of themselves went with it and it was never difficult to accept. Some could afford only the thought, or the personal service of working on or searching for something; and others could afford nothing but saying, at unexpected moments, "God bless you"—and there's no lovelier gift.

I began to write this yesterday, and yesterday brought the worst snowstorm of this year of 1962—almost as bad as that February one last year. The snow began the night of the thirteenth and on Valentine's Day was a welter of white—wet, heavy, and inexorable. Somehow the rural carrier got through with the mail (mostly valentines); so did the milkman—two good friends we often forget to thank. A friend ploughed my driveway about one o'clock in the afternoon and another turned up at five to do some shoveling. Two close friends who were to be dinner guests decided to cancel and I managed to reach Gussie, who, together with her helpful husband, was just leaving her house to come to mine over the ploughed, but dangerous back roads. So I went on working and, when I was hungry, took an emergency ration from the freezer and made some coffee, and that was that. The snow was still falling when I went upstairs to watch television, wondering how long it would be before wires would go; they were freighted with snow, as was every tree, with lower branches bowed to the ground.

I made a TV tour of the White House with Mrs. Kennedy and after the news, which wasn't encouraging weatherwise, went to bed. I woke at one and could not return to the oblivion of dreams, so I went back to the sun porch and looked awhile at a late motion picture, one made thirty years ago—I remember when first I saw it. Then I prowled downstairs, taking my bedside flashlight, which, of course, went dead. If the current failed, I'd have to have a light to take me into the cellar to turn on the generator (I'm terrified of it), so I found new batteries and then went to the door to put on the outside light and see if it was still snowing. It was, in a lazy fashion, and you'd never know I'd been ploughed and shoveled out. I went back upstairs and stood for a time at the sun-porch windows, looking out on the strangest world—white, all white and there was no contrast, for the sky was white also. The only relief from whiteness was in the tops of very tall pine trees, which had, somehow, shed their snow.

This morning, when I came downstairs, I inspected the bird feeder closest to the house. It was under a great mound of snow, but at one side there was something that looked like a little tunnel; a really enterprising bird could fold his wings and creep in there where it's a little sheltered and where stray seeds might be found for the looking. Perhaps, when personal storms overtake us, we can find our own tunnel to warmth and nourishment.

Since then I've been ploughed out again and in the late afternoon there will be a re-shoveling. I have to speak tonight at a charity-organization dinner; I'm afraid I was hoping that it would be canceled, but it hasn't been. Someone is to pick me up and as she doesn't know the way and the roads are treacherous, I wonder. . . . I know one thing, however; it is no time for elegance and chic. I have an opposum coat which is twenty years old or more. It is split past repair and when, on bad days, I wear it, my friends look upon me with horror. But it is warm and no snow penetrates. Did I tell you I had pneumonia last December? Well, I did and I've no intention of having it again, so I shall put on the old coat, the battered storm boots, and stagger out to a car, hoping for the best (which, I may add, is all my audience can do).

The sun is trying to come out and a while ago, over a luncheon tray, I was thinking that, within each month, other months are contained, rather like the carved balls within balls, which Chinese workmen make. . . . I put myself back into last August, into a moment of pure delight when everything was forgotten except water, sun, and sand, as I walked on a narrow beach with a beautiful dog, who is my friend. She belongs to Gladys Taber who, when I visit her, shares her Irish with me. I also remembered standing under the cottage windows to look into the giving heart of the most lovely rose, the Spartan. Yet, during that August, there were also wakeful nights, when pressures and anxieties were as a tight, steel band about my forehead and I could not sleep or make decisions, or even, after prayer, find peace.

Each month somehow repeats another, not only in the vagaries of nature but in our personal thinking and feeling. Each brings enchantments and everyday living and loving, each its own experiences and problems, which we must try to meet and solve, always aware of quiet pleasure and of gratitude for beauty and supply and friends.

So, as I look back now to summer, I find it easy to recapture the enchantment and let the rest go. Is it not wonderful that in the chill of February we can look back—and forward—to the warmth of August?

This month the stirring of spring is apparent to the sensitive spirit; the eye cannot see beneath the iron-hard, snow-covered earth nor the ear really hear what the root is saying but, looking at the calendar, we know that somewhere there is, already, rosy bloom.

We're always talking and writing about the promise of spring in winter, but we rarely stop to think that it's really so and not just an attractively worded cliché. In recent years, however, I've considered it seriously, for winter is not only a season; it is also a cruel climate of the heart and mind. To be able to trust and believe in—for trust and belief are not always quite the same—the day of thaw, the new growth, the beneficent sun, is an ever-present help in time of trouble.

Anything can contribute to a spring-in-winter mood—an understanding friend, great words in an enduring book, the sound of music or laughter, the inner silence when the emotionally cold world holds its breath, a job that must be done, or helping someone in greater difficulty than yourself. I recall that just before the trees began to blaze with color last autumn, I was, within myself, in the dark of the moon. And then something happened. I received a letter, laboriously written in pencil. It was from a nine-year-old child who had heard her older sister speak of me. I'd never met either of them, but the sister was known to me through the rural school I sponsor in the South, and those children write me now and again. This little girl wrote me something her sister had said. I do not merit it, but my heart was lifted; and at the end of the letter the child added, "I am sending you my picture. I would like to have yours and I send my love, too."

Love is the theme of "Valentine's Day." It all began in honor of romantic love, but the makers of valentines have extended it to filial, parental, and all the relationships of blood and marriage and friendship—all being a part of the whole.

What the little girl wrote of me isn't true, never has been, never will be, but it was as if the thin curve of the new moon lighted my darkness, for if someone believed in me, I must believe in myself.

Who, save God, can contemplate and understand all the depths and heights of the human heart, mind, and spirit? We cannot. We try, and are sometimes permitted a little insight into other people's and even into our own. But each, in a sense, walks by himself, however much he is loved, and none fully comprehends the changes in his personal climate or moon phases.

Now, in the middle of February, whether it rains where you are, whether it's spring, midsummer, or winter—as the earth turns on its axis—happy Valentine's Day, many Valentines, and I hope all of you who were born this month of presidential anniversaries will blow out, with pleasure, the birthday-cake candles. And may you know, when you enter into a time of moon darkness, that it will be only a little while before the world is bright again.

It occurs to me that for the shortest month I have written a long chapter. But then I've always been inconsistent.

Now the sun is shining and the eerie white world is a brilliant white. And as the little girl sent me her love, so I send you mine.

Happy February.

I, February . . .

February brings us the palest blue sky after storm, and on clear evenings the scarlet sunsets are punctuated with gold and occasionally streaked with an extraordinary lambent green seen only in winter. I don't think I'd ever realized that before until I read a book called Precious Bane.

Valentines come to us in February, a harvest of sown love and friendship and we need not keep them until they grow dusty and dog-eared to remember the glow they brought. The month also gives us the companionship, in thought, of great men whose contribution to the country in which we live was incalcuable, and those words are legacies.

Now, too, we harvest January in sheaves of ermine, in handfuls of diamonds, and when the sun shines, the tree shadows form precise and lovely patterns.

Red suns setting, red paper hearts, red fires on the hearthstone and, hanging from the eaves, icicles like little crystal swords or the cut-crystal pendants of a chandelier—by all these tokens we remember February.

Watching, as I write, the heaven-blue horizon, and the

snow enhancing tree and bush, I think that February—this fifteenth day of it—has left me, in memory, a water-color painting lovelier than any I've ever seen.

I'll hang it on the walls of my heart's house and look at it, now and again.

So, thank you, February.

MARCH

WHAT can one say about March? When someone knocks, I say, according to the month's current temperament, "Come in—or blow in." I've been having screen-door trouble for quite a while. The thing has tantrums and won't shut unless you hold it firmly.

March is a marvelous month in which to be gloomy—at least where I live. One moment you say, "What a lovely day; you can smell the spring," and the next you are announcing, "Well, of course, some of our worst blizzards have been in March."

That's for sure. For instance, our regional blizzard of '88, of which I have spoken. Still my mother enjoyed it; she was a student at Normal School, training to be a teacher; that day, she didn't go; she couldn't get out of the house.

One thing I know about March—whether it storms or shines, it is the key to spring. It can be a sun-warmed key, or a wet one, or a cold; but a key just the same.

Two years ago this month, I flew off to Florida to visit a very dear friend in Sarasota, and after that, to cross the state by car and be with my older son on his birthday and that of his little girl, a day before.

The flight was, to say the least, confusing; it included three planes and, counting the time from the hour I left my house for the airport to the hour in which I tottered in at my hostess' door, the time consumed was from eight one morning, until one the next. As for basking on the beach once I had arrived, who basks in the rain? Ducks? Frogs? I am neither. And when I reached the place where my son lived, it also rained. On his birthday, we watched through a large window an aquacade performance in, and around, the hotel pool. It was not raining, at the moment, but the pretty girls in fetching bathing suits were blue with cold.

Never trust March. That year I left for home in rain, and landed in snow.

Last year I flew back to my friend's enchanting house, leaving Idlewild with a heavy cold, during a rain, snow, and sleet storm, and arrived in Florida when the temperature was 85 degrees. Mine was higher. I had what is known as walking pneumonia, but I kept on walking and not until I reached the place where my daughter-in-law lived did I succumb to seeing a doctor, a delightful woman who looked at me and said amiably, "I'd like to listen to your chest."

I said, "Go ahead, if it gives you any pleasure."

It didn't.

This year I'm off again to visit my childhood friend in Sarasota and then to my daughter-in-law's. When I reach my last stopover in Florida, my daughter-in-law and I will go on to Bermuda. . . . But I can't tell you about that now; I haven't been there yet.

All months, all seasons, occasionally produce the unexpected, but with March, the unexpected is routine. Sometimes she's forgetful, identifies herself with Halloween and rides in on a broomstick. When she gets where she's going, she uses the broom with vigor, sweeping twigs from trees, leaves from hiding places, and dust out of corners. When I enter my house, she comes along right through the door and sweeps in with me a few of last year's overlooked leaves.

Now and then she appears, like April, in a sun-dazzled shower, or, masquerading as May, she brightens an hour with a shaft of warming light; often, disguised as February, she wears a cloak of snow.

If there is anything certain in this world beyond accepted death and taxes, it is the unexpected, occurring in a month, a day, or a season of unusual weather, or in the changeful climates of our personal lives.

Haven't you noticed? When matters seem to be running more smoothly than you'd hoped, when the road you are on —literally or figuratively—is pleasant and delightfully landscaped, all of a sudden there's a sharp turn, a ditch, a fallen tree—an obstruction. It happens to everyone, but it can also —thank heaven!—happen the other way round. When the going is rough and the mind tires and the strength fails and you wonder how you can, so to speak, drive another mile, again the unexpected happens—the storm clears, the road turns, the light pours down, and things are right again.

Most of us try to save a little, materially, against disaster, against the unforeseen drain on the resources or for something we greatly desire and cannot yet afford. It's a good idea, also, to save spiritually, building up a reserve against difficulties, a private bank account of inner fortitude and of trust, so that when we run head on into a crisis, when the blow falls and the world darkens, we have something to draw upon which will see us through; courage, for instance, to meet responsibility and sorrow, the belief that, however dark the moment, the sun will shine once more.

Only through trust and the knowledge that the accounts are always balanced can we achieve serenity. We all fall very short of our spiritual goals, just as we fall short of our material ambitions. But there are only a few basic truths and they have been taught over numberless years, in all religions: love and trust, and do unto others as you would be done by. Were everyone in this spinning, troubled world to practice these principles, it would no longer be troubled.

It is not difficult to pray in the quiet of one's own room or the peace of a church, a temple, a chapel or a shrine; it is simple to withdraw for a few minutes from the world about one. But to carry this attitude into the kitchen and the living room, to take it with us into the office or shop, to walk with it on a street, to enter—bearing it with us—the houses of friends or strangers, is very hard, indeed. But I believe that the least effort counts.

It must not be a self-conscious effort. The person who goes about deliberately dispensing kindness and understanding, who thinks of himself as going the second mile, or as rigidly obeying certain principles and, therefore, earning merit, has earned very little. To be sure, what he does for others counts—the seeds that are sown do not always fall upon stony soil—but to be spiritually smug and consciously noble is no star in anyone's crown.

The spontaneous, unegotistical giving, of which the giver is really unaware, is as natural and as easy as breathing. And it is, indeed, the very breath of the spirit.

When the unexpected happens and we learn to draw upon our hidden reserves, we find that we are able to extend ourselves in the effort to understand the multiple difficulties of others. Some people just retreat behind the walls of their own personal problems, they sit in a corner of themselves and whimper; others, recognizing themselves as part of a universal family, find that the problems which beset them draw them closer to friend and stranger.

This is belonging to the Family of Man.

All living has its seasons of storm, of sun, of drought and harvest. These are not arbitrarily divided as in the calendar year. Who among us has not known someone young who seemed to exist in an atmosphere of perpetual winter, and someone old who appeared to live surrounded by eternal spring?

When I go South again this month, no matter what the weather is or what the delays en route, I am sure of some things: of a warm welcome in a house which looks out upon the Gulf, a very short stroll from the beach and the peacock waters; a house with a fireplace flanked with hand-made ceramic tiles representing things I love, fish and shells and seahorses; a house with flowers outdoors and in; a blue-tiled pool, a patio, verandas, birds, and a lagoon. Perhaps one plane will be all I'm required to take; possibly the weather will even be kind when I fly; maybe the beach will be warm and golden, and the wonderful Southern spring will have taken over; there may be roses in the garden, and flowering bushes. Perhaps not; it doesn't matter. It's the welcome that is important.

And when I go to where my daughter-in-law lives, it may be hot or cold, it may rain, it may not; but she'll be there and the children, and Bermuda will be ahead. It's not easy to get to Bermuda from her nearest airport. But, who cares?

To expect trouble is dangerous and foolish; to be prepared for it is merely a safety measure. To fear the unexpected is natural enough, but to meet it with one's personal reserves is an overcoming.

Recently, a friend suggested that I should write about keys. It appeared that I'd mentioned them too briefly for her in another book. She gave me chapter and paragraph, but I didn't look up the reference, for I have a fearful aversion to reading my own books once they've been published. However, I like to think about keys.

Let us consider the key to outer space. Last month, on the twentieth to be exact, I sat spellbound before my television set for hours, until my eyes nearly fell out of my head and my senses reeled, watching the first American to go into orbit. The keys to that achievement were courage and determination, years of training, armies of scientists and technicians, and long hours of patient, painstaking work; also disappointment and failure and trying again.

Sometimes I visualize mortal life as a long corridor—you can't see the beginning of it and you can't see the end. There isn't any end, of course, just another corridor about which you know little or nothing. But this one called "living on earth" is long and wide, and all you can really see are myriads of doors, each opening into something important. And for each of them you must find keys. Two, labeled environment and heredity, are put into your hands when you are born. The others you must forge for yourself, sometimes with enthusiasm, always with gravity and care, and, very often, with pain. So, you make mistakes. You try a key and it doesn't fit. Then you must make it over.

Call the doors anything you want to. I call them by many names. There is one which opens to "courage" and it takes quite a while to make the right, smooth-fitting key for that, forged as it must be in the fires of faith and trust.

There is a door called "work." This one certainly can't be opened with any old key; you may try a number and they may not open the door you want, but sooner or later, if you keep at it, you will, through perseverance and inner guidance, find the right one. There is also a door called "believing," and what you believe in isn't as important as the fact that you do believe in something. Sometimes you have to make any number of keys before one slips easily into the lock and you reach your security.

What about the door called "happiness"? you may ask. That one I cannot tell you much about. I just know that one person's happiness isn't like another's. We all have different standards and demands and hopes, so you may fashion a hundred keys for this as you walk down the long corridor of a lifetime. And some will fit and you'll go through the door, only to become restless after a while and go out again, looking for another door, another key. Eventually, if you're lucky, the right key will miraculously fit the right door, and you will enter a room in which you can live for the rest of your days.

The door called "love" is not a one-way door; it opens outward as well as inward. You have to have two keys, really, because this door has a double lock. One key will permit you to unlock yourself so that you can truly be loved; the other, more important, permits you to love someone else.

Oh, so many doors! The door of "pain" is important, and the key which fits it has been forged from the same material as the key which opens the door to "courage." There's a door called "learning," and its key can be made by anyone who wants it. Learning isn't wisdom, and it certainly does not lie only in books or formal education; it is, simply, what you derive from living.

I suppose that the most important door is the one which opens on "spiritual understanding," which is also compassion and far more than that. I doubt if many people learn, while young, to make the key which fits this. It takes a long and often lonely walk down the corridor to discover the material that goes into such a key. But once you have made and used it, nothing which affects you personally can deeply trouble you again—neither your own sorrow and fears, nor the world's increasing disturbance and tensions —but other people's anxieties will reach you, and no one is wholly detached from trouble which afflicts someone he loves.

The key to spiritual understanding unlocks the ultimate door. Beyond it, there are vistas beautiful to contemplate. At its threshold all prejudice and selfish terror vanish. Those fortunate enough to have manufactured this key from ingredients known only to themselves, must find, on entering this door, the only sanctuary this side of heaven, a small portion of the peace which passeth earth's understanding, a little glimpse of the path upon which our stumbling feet are set; a different path for each of us but leading to the same eternal goal, the ultimate knowledge of God. . . .

So, now it's March. Last month I was talking about an early spring; and on the day of the Man into Space I looked out upon mounds of snow and birds searching beneath the feeders for nourishment. I looked out on branches and twigs iced over, though the sun shone too brightly for long looking; a fragile and brittle world, glittering and, in its way, cruel; for much of the big burning bush at my door had been destroyed and the branches of the big pines were freighted with frozen snow; the lower ones held fast in mounds of snow upon the ground. Early spring, indeed!

Yet March is spring's key, however cold or heavy it feels in the hand. Let's turn it in the door—there are twelve of these doors, remember, every year—and go on in. Whether it opens on snow or rain, wind or calm, sunshine or blowing darkness, it is the beginning of the springtime, the very threshhold of April.

This year, barring the unforeseen and acts of God, I

shall step from March into a Southern spring, even into a beginning of summer, into places once visited and loved, into a place I've as yet not seen, and come back home, at the end of the month to polish up the key for April and whatever it may bring.

Last month brought the Chinese New Year, the Year of the Tiger; some year will be, I hope, the Year of the Dove. I've already heard the mourning doves' plaintive note. It is a hopeful omen, a dove singing in the snow, and a joy to look from the dove to a white-iced branch with a cardinal swinging, red as flame, upon it.

I, March . . .

March has brought me a real harvest. For a long time I've been sowing hopes and plans. Now I look back at Sarasota revisited—sunlight and flowers and, for the third year in a row, the companionship of Janet the First; old friends and new; lazy days; a heron standing on the bank of the lagoon; and the calm or stormy waters of the Gulf, creaming at the edge of the sand.

It also brought me a glimpse of the grandchildren whom I hadn't seen for a year; and then, Bermuda—the trip, my daughter-in-law and I had planned together.

Here was a legacy, March's gift. Our rooms in the hotel at the water's edge overlooked a swimming pool and the bay beyond. There were old friends and new; exploring on foot and by car; ancient houses to visit—and I was nearly blown off the top of Fort St. Catherine in high Bermuda wind. There were new things to see and do, change and rest, and all around us the incomparable beauty of the little island.

Then home, by air, to March's further gifts of sapphires

spilled in puddles of water after hard rain, to frozen clumps of snow and my pond ruffling in spring breezes.

March bequeaths a stirring under hostile-seeming soil; a gathering of birds—the redwing, the robin; and the certain knowledge that, with the sun higher and warmer, we go forward steadily into summer glory.

To me, personally, March has given birthdays to remember: my mother's, a cousin's, my older son's and his little daughter's, and close friends'. Every month reminds me it's someone's birthday. I don't think of anyone (except the very young) as being a year older, but rather as having experienced another harvest, twelve months of growth, like trees, standing tall and firm, rooted in earth but skyward-reaching.

March brings us St. Patrick's Day. This year I was not home to celebrate it and the birthday of a friend who deserves the luck of the Irish—bless them. I've always been glad that in my heritage I've one Irish ancestor. . . . Bless, indeed, all nationalities, all men.

Now at the end of March, I look back on happiness, on nostalgia, and on sorrow as well. But the world turns, and we look, with what courage we can muster, upon the dark side as well as the bright.

So, thank you, March.

APRIL

WHEN, in my neck o' the woods, Easter comes early this month (or late in March), it sometimes arrives in furs, and those, young and old, who have new suits or frocks for the rejoicing season must conceal them under heavy coats for church, and wonder, during the Easter parades, if the flowers on their bonnets will freeze. My grandmother always said, "Pride feels no pain," and I thought of that over thirty years ago when, in a brand-new gray flannel suit (long before gray flannel suits had any special significance) and a very funny, but fashionable hat, I sat shivering on top of a Fifth Avenue bus—open, of course—and hoped that, if pride felt no pain, it would also prevent me from getting pneumonia.

This year, Easter is late, but whenever it comes on the calendar, it is always a green, as well as a golden light, the go-forward-into-spring signal. Last month we had a week or so of very warm weather, and things began to pop. Not unexpectedly, this was followed by a slight freeze; sometimes I think you can't win, or not entirely. Anyway, before the capricious girl with the blue eyes and yellow hair made her entrance, hyacinths were in bloom under our south window. There was a lone jonquil, too; and three tulips which, while wide open, still seemed to huddle close to the ground. The maples displayed little red leaf buds and I could see on all the bushes a faint greening look.

More birds come now and I am certain that, this year, April won't bring a basketful of snow with her, to toss to the veering winds.

Actually, although I sometimes complain, I like a changing climate with its unforeseen ways. Not that I wouldn't wake up screaming if, toward the end of April, we should have a blizzard. I change my house around twice a year, but Nature changes her curtains and upholstery twelve times, so there's nothing monotonous about it in this section. Of course, winter is sometimes too long; spring is always too short; and summer can be anything.

I've lots of crocuses in the grass; they look up like little stars, white and purple and yellow. The trick of planting a camphor ball and a clove of garlic with every bulb seems to have worked out, but I still have one ancient and wily mole who tunnels about and does as he pleases. Perhaps he has no sense of smell.

In this month, my twins were born, numerous friends, and also my sister. Upon her birthday I also have a little special anniversary. I celebrate it alone, but I shall never forget it; I have my sister's personal new year to remind me.

Now, as the peepers chorus, we'll surely have great, wonderful skies of stars and amateur gardeners will be looking for rain and worrying about a late frost. Most professionals here don't plant until about the tenth of May. Some people raise seedlings in little greenhouses—we used to—

mature them in cold frames, and then plant. But it's always an anxious time.

All winter long, home gardeners have been reading seed catalogues and longing for the iron clasp of frost to loosen, so they can go out and make their mudpies. These gay catalogues are a form of escape from winter.

All of us endeavor, by one means or another, to escape from tedium, the daily routine, annoyances, and from whatever comes to us in the way of grief or disappointment; we also try to run from fear and anxiety. For man, the egotistical animal, inhabits his own world of self and truly escapes from it, during his mortal lifetime, only in moments of nobility. The majority of us are self-centered; even when we deeply love, the self is concerned. And some people never seem to get outside themselves even for short periods of time. What happens to each of us seems paramount. And when it is unhappy, we utter the despairing, astonished, universal cry: "Why me?" There is no brief answer . . . there is no one answer. Sometimes, if we are objective, we can trace cause and effect, but there are times when we cannot and there seems to be no answer at all.

One reason so many people resent the inescapable fact of eventual, physical death is that, even though they may not believe it to be oblivion—and those who believe in Easter know it is not—they cannot conceive that this little world will go on without them. When I was young, I used to wake in the night, literally shaking with fear—or was it anger?—lest the day dawn and I'd not, on earth, be able to see it.

This season clearly demonstrates that everything goes on; after winter, there is spring.

Men's private self-worlds are rather like our geographical world; seasons, storm and sun, deserts, oases, mountains and abysses, the endless-seeming plateaus, darkness and light, and always the sowing and the reaping.

When our personal world is dark, we seek to fix the blame on any one of a number of factors—heredity, parents, destiny, what is known as bad luck or the bad break, and occasionally even on God.

It takes a long while to learn that sometimes we, ourselves, put out or, at least cloud over, our own sun, and that all things balance in the end. In nights of darkness we forget the shining days, though everyone experiences both.

I had a friend who was bountiful in her giving, a remarkable mother and godmother, honest, frank, original in her expression; it was a joy to be with her. She suffered from a serious cardiac disorder and had severe pain during her frequent attacks. I saw her at church shortly after one of these, and she said to me that she hated pain, she deeply resented it, but that, during her attacks she prayed for everyone, everywhere, who was also, at that moment, in pain.

I've not forgotten. If, when we are in pain or sorrow, anxiety or trouble, we can leave the self world long enough to pray for friends and strangers in similar situations, we have taken a small step closer to the basic truth of brotherhood.

Last year—or was it the year before? Time plays tricks with me nowadays—I went to the Sterling Forest Gardens again. I'd been there during the previous autumn, when late roses and annuals were in bloom. This time I went to see the upthrusting beauty of a million bulbs in flower. It was, I think in May. I am sad that I won't be going this year with my two good friends; one of them, who provided the car and did the driving, has moved to Texas. But that was a wonderful outing. We stayed in the motel which was designed by a Japanese architect; we had a whole day at the gardens, walking slowly and with enjoyment, looking at fountains and tulips, watching men work on the rose gardens which would bloom later.

It seems to me that few people walk their ways with deliberation, stopping every so often to delight in the seasons and in the simple, important, enduring things. Most of those I know are either rushing about blindly, almost headlong, or inching along, looking down. Both methods of progression are, in a spiritual sense, not progression at all, but symptoms of fear.

No matter what has happened or what you fear will happen, you have to walk as though you were going somewhere—not in a hurry, not at a crawl, and certainly not running away from something toward you know not what.

It cannot be said too often, or by too many people, that the path we follow must be taken a step at a time—never on the run, and never standing still, neither going backward nor marking time. Everyone hazards a guess at the future—his own, the future of those he loves, the future of the country and the world. Statisticians often come up with some amazing suggestions; so do computers; but no one really knows. Only He knows, Who created this world in all its beauty, and our small selves, with it. And it's just as well that we don't know.

I know, of course, that tonight friends are to come to dinner and tomorrow I'm to have my hair done and meet other friends for lunch, and that I have an engagement with still another for dinner out and a movie. I'll go to church on Sunday; and on the following Wednesday I am scheduled to talk to a group of women at a nearby church. There has to be certain amount of planning and I try, though my engagement calendar is apt to be pretty well mixed up. Sometimes, when I am asked to speak, I write down the name of the place (but not that of the chairman of the program) or the name of the chairman (but not that of the place).

Well, plans don't always work out. Between now and seven the telephone may ring and my friends tell me that, after all, they can't come—and I'll have to break the news to Gussie, who has also made plans in her department. Maybe tomorrow something will prevent me from going to the beauty shop, or from seeing the movie. Perhaps on Sunday—or next Wednesday—the cough which has plagued me for a month will be worse. Who knows? But, unless an ax falls somewhere in my family, probably nothing drastic will have happened. I'll just postpone the engagements if I can, that's all.

I think that too often we do not make—and keep—private engagements with ourselves. No matter how busy or pressured we are, we can engage ourselves to be alone for a little while each day, to go somewhere quiet and apart, where telephones won't ring, where we can look out of a window and be still, within ourselves. This is as good for the tumultuous mind and the spirit as the nap is for the physical body; but few of us have time enough for naps.

I remember an old German woman, whom I knew and loved when, from 1914 to 1917, I lived in her country. *Grossmutter* would lie down and nap every day, after the noon dinner. Twenty people could be there, but her routine was not interrupted. Apparently, however, she did not want to miss anything even in her sleep, so she would dispose of herself upon an uncomfortable-looking couch in her parlor, put a large, white handkerchief over her eyes, and drift into slumber. At the end of exactly twenty minutes, she would sit up briskly and inquire what had been said during her temporary absence from the general conversation. Meanwhile, we hadn't even lowered our voices as that, she said, would have kept her awake. She'd made a physical engagement with herself, and told me that she'd kept it faithfully for over sixty years. If she went out during the day, she simply made her engagement for just before, or just after, supper.

But the engagement with yourself that I recommend is a spiritual one and if anxiety intrudes, tell it to go away and come back again at, say four o'clock tomorrow.

That is not an original idea with me. I had a physician whom I dearly loved and, shortly before his death, I said to him that I was sick and tired of worrying. "Well," he prescribed, "when it gets bad, tell it to go away and come back later. But stipulate when, and keep that engagement."

He knew, I suspect, that a little respite gives a new perspective, but also that you have to face up to things; you can't say, "Go away, forever."

Fear seems to set the tempo of the times. Since man first learned to stand erect, he also learned, slowly and painfully, that the head-high, shoulders-back outlook upon life is the only one which takes us along the path; not always smoothly, but at least we keep on going and after a while we learn to set our own pace, neither panic-fast nor snail-slow. I fully realize that much of the fear which has tormented us—particularly in recent years—is for other people. Folks like me, who are old, are mainly concerned with those who are young. But fear has never cured or alleviated any situation—and never will.

This Easter season, like every other, is a pledge. Even if it suddenly snows, the hours of sunlight increase, and, barring rare blizzards, April snow is not a threat but a benediction—for there are chemicals in it, we're told, which nurture growing things.

My heart goes on tiptoe, looking through the thin green veils of April into May. I won't have gardens of my own, as once I did; only the bulbs leaping up in the half-moon bed under the south window, the color of crocuses in the grass, and the small, wild things down in the woods, where, later, there will be flowering bushes and carpets of violets. Here on Fable Farm the soil is rather unfriendly and there isn't much of it. Beneath the meager layer of topsoil we have sand and gravel. Once, I suppose, this part of the world was under the waters of Long Island Sound (before it had a name).

Anyway, we'll sow some grass seed, hopefully, and see what we harvest. I am one of the few people who do not shrink with horror from sun-faced dandelions in the lawn. In that respect I do not take after my father. At our country home he was apt to give his guests—weekenders, overnighters, or just stop-by-for-lunchers—a large, satisfying meal and then thrust trowels into their hands and bid them go out and destroy the dandelions. The lawn at old Hilo was remarkable anyway, being studded with apple trees, for he could not bear to cut down a tree which still lived.

This month I have several speaking engagements (I spoke to one group last night) and in May there are four more. I accepted the fourth this morning, principally because I was called early and was still half asleep. So now I look forward to Philadelphia in a few weeks. At least, I look forward to seeing old friends and new, but train trips, which I rarely undertake, disturb me.

Looking forward is not, as some insist, a form of escape, unless, of course, you live entirely in the future. But in the ordinary way of things it's a declaration of abiding trust.

All light requires fuel, except perhaps the celestial—and don't the scientists talk about gases even there?—the flint and stone set to wood, the match to the candle, the oil to the wick, the current running through the wires. The lovely radiance of granted prayer also requires fuel—trust, that into darkness there will come light.

Whether this Easter in your part of the world is warm or cold, whether it snows or rains or shines with sun, whether the flowers are budding or have already bloomed, you can trust in the Easter promise.

In dusk or dawn of this blowing, whimsical, April weather I think back—as I do each month—over times past, which have brought to me, as to almost everyone else, a share of difficulty, sorrow, personal anxiety, and frustration. Yet I'll not think of these, but remember isolated pictures—a sunset one November night which was a glory of gold and scarlet and masses of mauve-pink clouds; a Christmas tree; the rustle of palms in another state; the view of the harbour in Bermuda and lilies coming into bloom. I shall remember, too, a summer of almost intolerable heat and the look of silky, blue water under a blazing sky. All that we see and hear stays somewhere in our consciousness and the smallest thing—a word read or spoken, a fragrance—will serve to trigger memory.

Look back upon winter with gratitude. Spring is the harvest of the darker months—everything you know starts to grow in darkness. Don't write and tell me that winter brought you only colds or the ubiquitous virus. Perhaps it did bring those (and to me as well). Who goes through the chilly months unscathed? But it also brought things not to be forgotten—silver moons and snow, brilliant under stars; it brought Christmas and a new year, and to each of us something happy, something unexpected, which was not another problem but a joy. For the pendulum swings; nothing is static; and the road, however long, does turn.

Late last year, I spoke to a group of young married people, all its members very perturbed about the world in which we live, about problems which, of course, might affect their private worlds. I could give them no easy answers. Having lived for a few months past sixty-eight years, and having been a professional writer for over forty of them, has not endowed me with special wisdom. I don't know any how-to-do or solve-it-yourself formulas. I know as little as these young folks about the future, and I could tell them only to bend with the wind and lean upon the spirit.

As the road turns toward Easter, turn with it, whatever your geographical or emotional climate. The spirit within each human being is a small fragment of the Divine and Eternal, and if we give it the opportunity to speak, it will do so—but only when we keep our engagement to dismiss everyday difficulties, be quiet, and listen.

Easter symbolizes the spirit within—the promise, growth, and wonderment. There's too little wonder in the world. We marvel at science, at men into space, at tall buildings, and man's success. But the real wonder lies all about us, as it always has, in the fallen leaf and in a flake of snow, as well as in the first flower, the first unfolding leaf bud of any spring.

At this month's end, many of our states turn their clocks ahead. We do, here in Connecticut, and I love the longer days, the lavish light. But perhaps, when we consider daylight saving, we should ponder what are we saving it for—this daylight. For it is to treasure, and to work with, not to squander and fritter away.

Going forward into any new season, God moves in a mysterious way and we with Him. May His promise, this returning spring, bring you joy at the Easter and the Passover seasons.

I, April . . .

April brings us the harvest sown in March and promises that of May. The most unpredictable of months, she gives us a rerun of her predecessor and a preview of her successor.

Her legacy is sunshine through showers, laughter through tears. March is more serious, a little hastier, and sterner about her house-cleaning duties. April winds are not as brisk, but she manages to stir up those twigs and branches that March overlooked and the last of the old, brown, rustling leaves.

Now we also harvest winter which has done its untidy, inexorable best with storm, wind, lashing rain, and the heavy white of snow. March has shaken her touseled head and done something about the leavings; April finishes the work, so that everyone is out, in back or front yards, wrestling with the debris.

It would be a more than unhappy world if people didn't go on doing as they've always done when seasons change: rake leaves or shovel snow; clean up, and replant. If everyone sat down and decided he'd wait for something terrible to happen, the whole machinery of the world would stop.

April leaves a legacy of beginning bloom and new color, of birds tuning up, of brooks running free. Each month is a stepping stone to the next, and this one, taking us into May, has left us treasure and the promise of more.

Topaz and pale jade, turquoise and amythest, the jewels of April, spilling over.

So, thank you, April.

MAY

♛

May is a month upon which we believe we can rely, yet, a year ago, I gave an outdoor picnic for my children and their children and we almost froze to death, except those young enough to keep running between snatches of frankfurters and hamburgers.

If May lives up to her good name, there's nothing sweeter than her mood, gentle, yielding, the winds subdued to a sighing, the sun not yet too warm—although it was on my sister's wedding day—and the blossoms opening before your very eyes.

As April is the stepping stone to May, so May is the stepping stone between uncertain spring and beautiful summer.

We're a long way from Christmas, in May, aren't we?—whether we figure forward or backward. Or are we? Time has a way of sliding fast, as if it were on a toboggan, and I've reached the place where I think ahead and also back, not only to Christmas but to birthdays. For giving is for all year round, whether in thought, imagination, or reality.

I've a friend whom I've never met who often sends me

things. First he sent me my own books to autograph for friends of his; then gifts just for me: a plant, a box of candy —how did he know I don't count calories?—or a magazine subscription.

And I've another friend, whom I see very often, who never comes to the house without something in her hand as well as in her heart. And whenever she goes on a trip she brings something back for me—not for a special day, just for giving's sake—and she says, "I brought you this from Toronto," or Miami or upstate or Bermuda, as the case may be.

So it's my birthday every time she comes.

Everyone can give of themselves; of warmth and hope and courage. Everyone can offer a shoulder for someone to cry on. Most of us have terrible moments of insecurity; all of us know hours of desperation and despair. And who among us doesn't know someone at this very moment who is ill, or in sorrow, or lonely? Everyone in this world, in whatever environment he lives, rich, poor, young or old, can use a little more hope, a little more love and understanding. They aren't difficult to dispense. There's a telephone nearby, which you can use to say, "I've been thinking of you"; and there's a pen somewhere at hand and a sheet of paper and it doesn't take long to write and ask, "How are you?" Perhaps you haven't heard from someone for a long time, but the gap is easily bridged; all you have to say or write is: "I haven't heard. . . . I'm worried about you."

Just don't put it off.

Let me tell you something. One December, shortly before Christmas, a young man I knew left his house to get into his car and go to work. It was raining that day in the South, a dismal day. He came back and asked his wife, "Is there any coffee left?" and she said there was, for in that house the coffeepot was rarely empty. So he sat down. She poured him a cup and one for herself and they drank it together, companionably. And suddenly he said to her, in effect, "Look, we've had rough times in many ways, but we're together. I just want to say how happy I am in our marriage and how much I love you and our children."

She went with him to the door and he said, "Don't worry, I'll drive carefully. I'll see you tonight." He kissed her and went out.

He did not return.

And what sustained her . . . after the telephone rang . . . after she knew . . . was that quiet, unexpected, spoken recognition of all they had shared for almost fifteen years. And as she said to me later, "That wasn't like him—at nine in the morning." Nor is it like many men. After dinner, yes; perhaps when the kids are asleep and you're sitting together, over coffee; or during the night when you wake and speak lovingly and drowsily to the person beside you. But not at nine in the morning, going off to work.

Always remember this. Preach it from the housetops; tell those who occupy actual pulpits to do so; tell it to your young friends and your old. . . . *Say that word of appreciation before it's too late.*

It doesn't have to be as grave as that, but it should be every day. Living is so confused and hurried . . . a man goes off to work a little late; a woman has the household to see to, a day to plan; the children have their own interests; all have problems. Except in a few relaxed moments or an emotional one, how few take time from their daily living to speak the small, the important word!

It takes so little time for a man to pat his wife on the shoulder and say, "You're the greatest," or maybe, "We have something special," or just, "Wasn't yesterday fun?" A woman can lean against her husband for a split second and say, "I wouldn't change you for anyone in this world." How much time does that take? None, really. And such recognition should not be reserved for the special moments; it should be as much a part of everyday living as sunrise and sunset.

We grow accustomed to our parents and we forget, quite soon, childhood and growing up, except what may have hurt us or what was unpleasant. So we became impatient or careless. Is it so hard to say often, "I remember all you did for me, the sacrifices you made, the love you gave"?

Is it so difficult to tell a child, "No matter how much I scold, I think you're wonderful," or just, "I'm so proud of you." Is it hard to tell a brother or sister, "Maybe we've disagreed sometimes, but what would I have done without you"? And is it unheard of to tell a friend how much you value his friendship?

Yes, say it before it's too late. Most people go out of a door and return in a matter of hours or days. Some do not. And if it has all been said, and many times, one who never again sees that door open—in a special way—has a sustaining knowledge, an inner strength.

We hurry so, we are so pressured. All these appreciative things are in our hearts, but we don't take the time to say them. Yet we take time to read a newspaper, watch TV, listen to the radio or talk to someone on the telephone about next month's bazaar or next week's organization meeting. I deeply feel that communication with those we love is one of the most important things in the world. Do it now—not in measured, solemn session but almost casually, because it will be a part of every day, if, every day, you say it.

This is the time of the year when I begin to look for Christmas presents. Most people think I'm demented and maybe they're right. But if I see something and can afford it, I buy, and put it away. In early April, I found a very special gift for a daughter's birthday which comes in July. Maybe I'll find something this May for a Christmas giving. It's always been hard for me to divide time into calendar months and as I grow older every month is extra dimensional, Christmas seems to be yesterday and Fourth of July tomorrow. Half of delight lies in remembering backward and the other half in hoping forward; and between the two halves, in the present moment of time, the whole is made.

It's a good idea really. I look out at May and the apple blossoms blowing, like snow, from the trees and the ivory white of dogwood, and remember the snow which falls from the winter sky.

To live in one's personal past, either nostalgically or resentfully, isn't a good idea, any more than it's good to live in an unreal future of wishful thinking; but to separate the months into remembered loveliness—that can be joyous.

Year long, the pleasantest things happen to me, without regard for calendars. Another giving friend of mine, who lives in California, sends me many packages—little gay things or something treasurable of her own, not bothering with special dates, although those, too, she remembers. So there's always something of her around, on my desk, in the living room or, at the properly festive time, on tree or table.

A while back, I spoke of the friend who brings me presents from afar, but I forgot to say she also comes lugging enormous shopping bags full of things she feels I might need (I always do) and haven't had time to shop for (I rarely have). From a Toronto trip one summer, she brought me the loveliest handkerchiefs I ever saw, for show, not for blow, and when I carried one to a ball—I hadn't been to a ball in thirty years—a couple of Decembers ago, I was right back in the middle of June with her.

May is a lavish time, everything spills over—the trees, the gardens, the shrubs. Gussie and my friends Alma and Agnes always share their gardens with me. I haven't much in the way of home-grown flowers and often think wistfully of the forty-five lilac bushes we had at the first Fable Farm—there are a few here, too—and always, every lilac time, I remember a circle of lilacs beside the little outside laundry building at my father's place on Shelter Island. They'd been planted that way, and grew tall and thick and almost merged but I could, as a child, squeeze myself in, somehow, and stand there in the center, hemmed in on all sides by the branches, and so enraptured by perfume that it was the way I'd think of heaven.

Giving is such fun; sharing's even better. People often send me fruit and cookies and all kinds of homemade jam and jelly, preserves, and whatever. Living as I do, alone, I can't consume it all myself, and I don't have company every night in the week. But I can share it with others.

Giving is one of the secrets of springtime, the sharing of bloom and fragrance and of life itself. May is a harvest of loveliness. If I leave the typewriter now and go to walk by the pond, there will be the May midges. But nothing is entirely perfect, I daresay, and they, too, are entitled to their life in the sun and in the lovely violet dusk. There should be a frog or two about; the peepers are still with us; and the birds, weary from their busy nest-building, are going sweetly to sleep. There may be rain in those darker clouds, this evening, but we need it.

May is not pressured; she has never heard of tension;

she's busy only with her own secret growth, which flowers into giving. She has her own way of expressing gratitude to God . . . and what is any human love but just that, a flowering toward the Creator?

Nothing is static. There is life everywhere—in the earth, the rain, the sunlight; in the very stones about us, in the walls which harbor us, in the tree which shelters. We do not live like flies caught in amber—yet who shall say that in their way they do not live?—but move with Nature, which goes forever forward. The stars and moon and sun, the earth we walk upon, which is also a planet—these are upon their appointed courses; and when winter binds the soil in icy chains and leaf and bud seem to sleep, they do not really, for every blade of grass, each branch and root is occupied in its speechless way with going forward.

The English novelist, Marie Corelli, once caused a character in Thelma to say that he did not believe in eternity as the future, for he possessed it now.

And so he did, for time, like a circle, is unending, and therefore it is the simplest thing in the world to look out upon May bloom while looking back at pine trees and snowstorms and ahead to the fruiting of September—remembering all the seasons, and recognizing their continuity.

Weather patterns change and we speak of good winters and bad, or early spring and late. We are resigned, I think, to the temperamental vagaries of the seasons, knowing that, beneath the variances, continuity remains.

I am certain that this May which, during its thirty-one days, may blow hot or cold or both, will keep certain promises, made not only in April but much longer ago than that. I am sure the lilacs will be sweet with heavy purple bloom and the fruit trees—despite the astonishing fact that a few in my section bloomed unseasonally last December—will burst into skyrocketing pink and white.

The gardens, planned last winter beside a hearth fire, will have been started and those who have planted them will hover and hope, water and weed. Boat owners will be haunting marinas and house-painting will be under way before it gets too hot.

And people—those who are thinking of moving, now, or in the autumn—will be out in even greater numbers than last month, looking at houses to rent or buy, or at new apartments.

The flags of this restless world have been tautly flying at the half-mast of tension for many years, but life goes on and May tells us so, in a shout of color. I remember some months ago, in a beauty shop, a woman complained bitterly that her thumb was "ruined." She had not hit it with a hammer or caught it in a car door; merely, the newly applied nail polish had smudged. And I thought of the headlines in that morning's paper and wondered how, with the world on a cliff's-edge, anything as trivial as blurred red enamel on a thumbnail could so upset her. Yet not long thereafter, when I was to speak to a group of people, I found myself fretting because I'd been unable to have my hair done for the evening. I told them this and about the thumbnail and suddenly thought—and said—that it was, after all, marvelous that we could quite normally escape from the gravity of living in our era into trivial concerns.

And it is marvelous. No matter what the headlines say—and having no crystal ball, I don't know what they'll say tomorrow morning—everyday life goes on and we accept it: meals must be cooked, dishes washed, beds made, laundry done, children sent off to school. Time is always at a woman's heels, and at a man's, to say nothing of the youngsters, preoccupied with their Scouting, dancing classes and parties, their homework, their little leagues.

Each of us lives so many lives; the twenty-four-hour life of waking and sleeping, the life of home and family responsibility, and that of work, outside of home. Those of us who live alone, whose families are grown and gone, or who are occupied in doing for other people's families—we all lead half a dozen lives. There is the life of the extending interest in the world around us, of books and music, the life which lies outdoors; and there is always the inner spiritual life of meditation and trust. Love leads a life all its own, and all the lives we live are interlocking.

Each of us is part of a large pattern, just as this very small world is part of a universe, throughout which God's plan and purpose operate. No matter what men do to upset the balance of nature, the plan and purpose remain. I am aware that this does not seem true on the surface; yet I am convinced that it is.

May is a time for the heart and spirit to stretch their wings. Growth is all around us, and we, too, grow. The bird nests, heedless of storm or altering weather; the flower pursues, in scent and silence, its path to light.

I loved spring in the city. It has a special flavor—window boxes blooming on ledges, flowerpots on fire escapes, pretty clothes, pretty girls, and shop windows gayer than a fiesta. I used to love driving through Central Park at dusk—there was a time when I drove behind horses—watching the city light its windows, or standing on an Esplanade in Brooklyn and looking across the river at the beautiful skyline and the soaring temples of commerce, each window brilliant.

I loved the park and the restaurants which ventured outdoors, either in a backyard garden or under a sidewalk awning, as in Europe. There was a feeling of release, and of laughter, for spring comes to a city as certainly as to the country.

But I rarely go to the city any more, for something has been added to all this: no one strolls along a pavement these days to look at spring in flower boxes or shop windows. Everyone hurries and there is something in a crowded city which translates itself into a physical unease—a headache perhaps, or a painful knot at the back of my neck.

Here, it's quiet except for the occasional cars which pass, and the daytime sound of building somewhere—but they haven't built out the peepers as yet, or the sound of wind in new leaves and the speech of birds.

May, like every month, is for living, for taking each day as it comes, with gratitude for all that has been, looking ahead with hope and trust, and always remembering that now is your very own. Now is the time for giving the things no one can buy, things which are purchased only with the golden coins of the spirit.

Happy Maytime.

I, May . . .

May leaves us a legacy of gold and blue and all the glowing jewel tones. She brings us new life outside the windows, and also the urge to "do something" inside. This is the time of year when we turn the house back to spring, and toward summer, with the lighter materials, the cooler colors and less happy clutter. That my house is usually cluttered, I do not deny.

May also gives me the urge to have the terrace flower boxes planted, in pinks and violets, striped leaves and trailing ivy. Sometimes I want to do it too soon because I suddenly can't stand the look of the bare stones—although when they were covered with snow, I'd wished they were bare. However, someone generally restrains me.

Last March, before I returned from Bermuda, my friend Agnes brought forsythia into the house and forced it, so it was a cascade of sunshine yellow over the hearth when I came into the room on a cold and windy night. After that, April had its own way and May brought fountains of it, golden fountains, falling over the stone walls.

May has brought the promise of roses and has left with us the harvest of her generosity.

She gave to me thoughts of my father and my nephew whom I can only remember lovingly on their birthdays—but to my little niece I can send a gift and to my sister, on her anniversary.

So, thank you, May.

JUNE

Now it is time to take a look at June. Even here, inside the house, her coming is apparent, in the flowers, in the blowing white or green of curtains at the open windows, and the gaiety of chintz. I haven't altered the bookshelf top where some of the mugs stand. I shifted them around last winter when new ones came to me for my collection and put most of the white ones, ironstone, Meissen, and milk glass, on the mantel of the library fireplace.

I always assume, as does everyone else, that June is the month of brides. Then I cross my fingers. You think that June is bound to be beautiful and you forget the cold Junes, and the rainy ones, and those which came whooshing in on a heat wave. However, given the harvest of a bountiful spring, June seems bridal—the pink and white blossoms of fruit trees stirred by wind, petals drifting, and the lovely choirs of many birds.

June, being the traditional month of graduations, also wears a cap on her golden head and a gown over her wedding dress; and she carries a diploma as well as roses. But traditions aren't really arbitrary, for people do marry in every month in the year and there are graduations in February. As far as that goes I attended one last August. And in this wide country of geographical differences, roses grow somewhere, year 'round.

In this part of the United States we think of June as even-tempered, a month upon which one can rely, bringing glorious sunlight, gentle winds, and quiet rains. But it isn't always so, of course. I've known her to blow in cold as March or hot as August; she can blot out the stars with storm, and roll the drums of thunder. And sometimes her rain is not brief. Years ago, I planned an outdoor picnic in June, this one for grownups. But it rained—so there we were, indoors, in a house not geared to a picnic for thirty people.

I also recall an early June in Minnesota. When I left Chicago by train, the temperature was eighty-six in the shade; it was even a little warmer in St. Paul. That evening I drove into Minneapolis to speak and thanked heaven for air conditioning. When I left, to drive back to St. Paul, the temperature had dropped forty degrees and for the rest of the time I was there it was cold and it rained and rained. . . . Still—it was June.

Well, one of the things we learn as we go along is to adjust, not only to changes in weather or in plans—but to altering circumstances as well. You can't meet them by taking off a coat or putting one on, by turning on the heat or the air conditioning.

There are people who never adapt, no matter how long they live, and those who learn, little by little. I'm one of the latter. I wasn't born flexible, I suppose, or organized either. I had to become so, and I finally reached a point where I began to think (and to be told) that I was over-organized. It took me quite a while to learn that the world wouldn't end just because I couldn't be somewhere I'd planned to be, when I'd planned.

A middle course is best. There's always another engagement you can make or another plane on which you can fly.

That is the essence of Robert Burns's remark about the best laid schemes of mice and men. I've often wondered, however, what mice scheme about, aside from running around attics, scampering in woodwork, and looking for cheese.

Lots of people hold a fatalistic attitude toward involuntary changes of plans. "Perhaps I wasn't meant to go," they say. I can't quite go along with this; the blizzard which grounds the plane was certinly not devised by nature for preventing, say, eighty people from going to Florida.

Flexibility, whether inborn or superimposed, operates in many departments. It functions through our attitudes toward people and in the way in which we adapt to them. Not everyone we meet thinks as we do, or follows the same behavior pattern. When we encounter someone whom we like at first sight and sound, it's wonderful; but often a second look and longer listening bring a mental reservation. And when we meet someone to whom we take an instant, unreasoning dislike, another meeting, or a third perhaps, often discloses a potential friend.

God, I believe, intended us to bend with the sudden wind, and dig down deep with our very roots to withstand storm. Few people—none, really, whom I know—live all their mortal lives in the rosy climate of traditional June—sunny, gentle, dependable. Character is not built by a succession of sunny days or by continuous victory. It takes defeat to bring us, victorious, back into the sun again. And it takes problems to teach us that there are solutions, and these we must find and face.

I was astonished some time ago to have a reader write to ask me, "Are you for real?" It seems that she'd once read a small and bitter book I'd written out of a shattering experience which I deeply resented. She had suffered a similar experience and felt that what I wrote was sincere. (And so it was!) Therefore she could not understand why, in later years, I was not still locked in that particular prison; she could not believe I wasn't, and so assumed that if I were the person in the little book I couldn't be, for instance, the one in these pages.

But we are many selves, each of us, and because, in a sense a new one is born from the old, it doesn't mean that the new is not "for real" or that the old one wasn't.

Last winter, speaking to a delightful audience of young women, I was asked if I used a different personality for each story, book, or article I write, for, the questioner said, having read me often in a magazine series, she had to adjust herself to seeing me in person, as her mental picture was so dissimilar. I was a little taken aback. I don't think writers assume personalities—at least not many of them. If my reader had pictured me as moving efficiently about a kitchen, or sitting with my knitting and sewing, or surrounded by the very young, she must have been skipping sentences. I have never concealed the horrid facts that I can't cook, can't sew, haven't knitted since the First World War—when I did it very badly—and that I am as rarely as possible a baby sitter. Far from being the large motherly type, which she had comfortably thought me, I'm knee-high to a tall grasshopper, weigh ninety-eight pounds and, despite the creaking bones of advancing age, manage to get around faster than a lot of people.

I've said all this, but those sentences she must have skipped (or else didn't think they were "for real"), therefore, I fear I disillusioned her. Perhaps writers should be read, not seen.

When I write a story about gay young things, I do not leap up from the typewriter and go into the Twist. When I write about hospitals, I don't deliberately break a leg or spray myself with an anesthetic—and when I put a sheet of paper into this machine, I don't snap my fingers, mutter a magic formula, and change myself into something I'm not.

All of us have a hundred faces, attitudes, and facets of personality. I don't think anyone is all of one piece. We're more like the patchwork quilts I love, little bits and pieces, bright or dark, sewed together with the sometimes uneven stitches of experience. I don't suppose any two members of our families, or any two friends, see us with the same vision and perspective. I tried to explain this to the pretty girl in that audience, but I couldn't, for I haven't the remotest idea what I seem like to other people. . . . Well, sometimes they tell me, and it isn't at all what I think about myself. Which leads me to wonder what I do think, for I often don't know what I seem like to me.

"Know thyself" has been said a hundred thousand times, and most of us try . . . particularly those who are naturally introspective. But something always comes between us and a crystal-clear recognition, for the ego intrudes, at all times.

The various aspects of personality are, I suppose, evidences of flexibility, of an effort to adapt ourselves to others, while still preserving the integral core which is the basic self.

Look in the mirror. You know what you look like, insofar as a mere reflection can show you; all reflections being, it is said, a little distorted. But do you really know yourself completely—beyond your beliefs, opinions, likes, dislikes, prejudices and interests? Of course, you don't, any more than I do.

The path we each travel can be very dark, indeed; it can turn unexpectedly, and we can't see around corners. Most of us, I think, pray for more light upon our personal roads—not to see far ahead or to foretell the future, but to illuminate the next step, which is all we can take. No one goes along his road in seven-league boots.

The light is always there; we ourselves cause the obscurity, for we cast very long shadows: selfishness, envy, vanity, fear, unkindness—the list is endless, and we can all add to it. Sometimes we cast the darker shadow of despair which is, I believe, a sin. I do not think that in this world, we can help casting shadows, but perhaps by conscious effort—through prayer and hard work—we can, during our lifetimes, shorten the shadow and increase the light.

Each year I try to tuck pieces of the seasons I love into a corner of my mind and hold them there to relive again and again. I don't keep a diary—unless this book is, in a way, a sort of journal—and it's so very easy to forget. But most of us have experienced the sudden "flash-back" memory, and there are thoughts and ponderings, written and spoken words, important events and small daily episodes which deserve to be remembered—the unexpected joys, which shone for us like new stars, and the recurring expected things, which held a familiar beauty.

It would be wonderful if we could gather together all the loveliness experienced in a year and assemble it into something tangible; the reaped harvests, the jewel of many colors, the perfume which holds the scent of a thousand flowers.

One Christmas, I was given something which looked like a telescope. I expected to peer into it, shake it, and see little colored pieces falling into patterns. But it wasn't like that at all. It's a long tube, light in the hand, and there's nothing manufactured inside it. You just look through it at anything in the room or outdoors. Not being scientifically or mechanically minded, I do not know how the result is accomplished, but you see what is directly and actually in your line of vision, and everything splits up into the most marvelous colors, designs, and shapes—whether you're looking at the amythest crystal vase on the living-room desk, the pale pink curtains at the windows, or the aquamarine porcelain lamp.

Most of us find everydayness tedious, and often the mere routine of getting up and going to bed, of preparing meals, of going out to work—or even out to play—becomes monotonous. If we could just look at chores, things, people, everything, through some such enchanted telescope of the mind, which would break the accustomed patterns into new design and color and loveliness, we'd find it a great deal easier to live with ourselves.

At this moment, I'm looking at a typewriter. It's gray; it's useful; and when I strike a key—usually the wrong one—it hums quietly away at me. It won't do my work for me—we haven't quite reached that point yet, although they tell us that machines will one day be taught to think—but it faithfully records my trials, my errors, and my small successes, just as life itself does. I try to look at it, not as just a utilitarian machine with which I earn a living and keep in touch with friends, but as a sort of treasure house of words. There are so many beautiful words in every language. I think of words lying locked in this machine, waiting for me to release them, to muster them into some sort of sequence, to employ them to convey a thought, a picture, a recital of events as in a letter, or a narrative about imaginary people, also imprisoned here until I set them free. In short, I can, if I try, think of the typewriter as an instrument of the mind, just as I, myself, am the instrument of the Intelligence which has created, and moves through, us all.

Years ago I knew a young woman who liked to cook and I asked her why? She answered that many of the materials she used were beautiful. She was making a salad as we talked, I remember, and she spoke of the shape and colors of the lettuce—white jade, pale jade, and darker green—and of the firm crimson globes of the tomatoes and the golden length of the carrots. It would be very difficult for me to feel that way, although I admire and enjoy a salad as much as the next person, and admit there is a gay magic about a young radish and polished beauty in a smooth purple eggplant. No, of course, she didn't use eggplant in the salad, but she did use raw cauliflower—little curls of celery, too.

She was an artist, working creatively in her kitchen and enjoying what she did. I have often said that everyone in the world has a spark of creativity which can be expressed in innumerable ways—not just on paper or canvas, not only on a stage or through a musical instrument, but in the making of a salad, the fashioning of a frock, or the designing of anything from a ship to a cottage, from a bridge to a toy. And always in human relationships.

The neighbor who comes to see you when something special has happened and says, "I'm happy for you," and you see it shining in her eyes; the one who comes in times of grief and quietly brings you a gift—a casserole, a cake, or a basket of June roses—and who says "I'm sorry"—they, too, are creating; they are creating love and identification with you, their neighbor.

Never be afraid to say, and do, what is in your heart,

thereby releasing the spark, for sometimes it can become a flame by which someone you love—or someone you hardly know—can warm his hands for months to come.

In a few moments, a friend will come in to have supper with me, and I'll go outside with her and look hopefully at the grass—we have great difficulty growing grass, except for the variety known as "crab"—and we can walk down to the big willow near the pond and listen to the birds. There's an old stone bench there, now very lopsided, but it will hold us, and we can sit together awhile before Gussie calls us in, and tell each other what we remember of other Junes, and all that has happened in the week just past.

To sit on a bench and talk while the dusk creeps in on padded feet is a very ordinary thing. I do it quite often and, unless something unusual has been said, forget it soon thereafter. But from now on, I am going to look through a little telescope and try to see whatever I experience in the true design in which it was fashioned. For nothing is really commonplace.

And, now, let's go along with June, adapting ourselves to whatever may be her mood; her storms will pass and we can always remember the undefeated roses.

So happy June—and if she brings you a holiday—happy journey or happy staying-at-home.

I, June . . .

All the while May was on the spring stage, performing for us before the pale green curtains, June was waiting in the wings for her cue, knowing that when May danced out, she would put into June's hands a legacy—her flowers grown taller for June, her grass, grown greener—the harvest given and taken.

June, in turn, will leave a heritage of white clouds on the indigo sea of the heavens, jeweled bushes, and clustering leaves, grown heavier. She will shatter the crystal of little lakes with wind, and her rains will pour brook water, brown over rocks, cascading into pools. And the stretches of salt water we see in June will be pinned with sunlight and pearled with foam.

June is a generous month and I for one, shall miss her until she comes again, this harbinger of deeper summer.

Isn't there, in June, an extra touch of silver polish on the stars, and doesn't the moon, in all her phases, know exactly what's expected of her?

June, like the other eleven months, must bring to some

of us sorrow remembered or newly experienced. There is great poignancy, I think, in looking from depths of personal suffering upon a seemingly indifferent and very lovely world; it is the added thrust, the turn of the screw. It's no easier to be unhappy on dark, cold, bleak days, but they are more suited to sorrow's frozen heart.

But whatever June brings, I'm grateful for her and for all Junes gone by, each with its legacy, each with its harvest.

So, thank you, June.

JULY

♛

Now that we're up to our ears in July . . . whatever became of June? She just went back to wherever she came from and is biding her time there, working to make herself a new wardrobe for next year.

About five months ago, I thought that July—to say nothing of April, May, and June—would never come, what with blizzards, ice, part of the roof collapsing, resultant leaks inside the house, and being marooned for a while . . . and was it ever cold! Then, I was thinking about how —heaven willing!—I'd be taking off in March for Florida and Bermuda to see people I loved whom I hadn't been with for quite a while. I was intelligently convinced that spring would arrive and then summer, as they always have —but it just didn't seem possible.

Now, working on hot days with the shutters closed and fans muttering, I look back and wish I could have a snowbank for just a few minutes.

No one's ever wholly satisfied. Maybe the ideal climate exists on this planet, but I doubt it. Even if it did and we lived in it, we'd find ourselves with a whole crop of dissatisfactions and, of course, anywhere, and anytime, we'd wish for those things we'd like and don't have.

Everyone has unrealized dreams, and some—like myself—a silly, childish list of Wishful Thoughts. When I was writing a great deal of so-called popular fiction, I used to dream of prestige and glowing critical reviews—neither of which I've ever attained—and from there on it was only a dream step to the Pultizer Prize and, of course, the Nobel. Or—as the writer of a play bound to have a five-year run, an opening in London, and roadshows from coast to coast, I pictured myself in a white Paris frock, taking bows before a wildly applauding audience—well, why not a standing ovation? . . . That was a long time ago, and the nearest I ever came to it was a midnight showing of my first movie—a silent—with an audience who'd never heard of me and was much more interested in the parade of stars, producers, and columnists across the stage. Also my dress was black.

Along about that time, I felt that in order to win critical acclaim, I should abandon my trivial little yarns and work, for years, on something stark and Russian—something of the "isn't-life-terrible?" school. I admitted this recently to a group of clubwomen, and they looked at me as if I had lost what little mind I possess. But it was just a case of the grass is always greener on the other side of the fence, no matter what the month.

I can't think at the moment of anything I'd like, and can't have. . . . Oh, yes—I've never taken a world cruise, or been asked to dinner at the White House or tea at Buckingham Palace; also I've never been presented with a winning ticket in the Irish Sweepstakes.

Well, I'll get along.

Have you ever known anyone who didn't think he'd had "a difficult life"? I haven't. The phrase crops up in intimate, or general, conversation all the time, and it is not heard only from those who have suffered material depreciation, grief, or loss of work, or from those who have to scrimp and save, or those who are forced to perform the most back-breaking tasks in order to make the barest living. No. People who live in obvious luxury, who haven't, it would seem, a care in the world, have often said to me, "My life hasn't been easy."

Sometimes they tell you why: sorrow, disillusionment, or disappointment; miserable marriages; children whom they call "ungrateful"; and sometimes it's because they have no children. It gives me an odd feeling, however, to sit and listen to a woman I've envied a little talking about her hardships and her fruitless search for something to sustain her.

We're apt to think that those whom we call "famous" are exempt from many of life's ills. "Look," we cry, "at all the success and rewards." What do we really know about such an individual except through the newspapers? Everyone's subject to the same disasters, the basic ones: failing in the struggle, even after reaching the top; illness—one's own or someone else's; and always the persistent human sense of insecurity which reaches into every department of life.

Now and then, people remark that they envy me. Me? I regard them with sincere amazement. Then they go on to say that it must be so wonderful to live quietly in the country, to have outdoor beauty to look upon, to inhabit an old house surrounded by charming things, yet to travel occasionally and see strange places and meet new people.

Well, it is sometimes, of course; but it isn't *always* wonderful; not by a long shot; not any more than every day in any season is perfection.

It was beginning to grow dark as I wrote, so I just got up and banged the screen door a couple of times to ward off the bumbling insects. I've shut off the light over the door, for there's no one coming in this evening. And I closed the indoor shutters also, so that the moths would not destroy themselves against the big panes of glass. I hate to see the fragile, frustrated things beating themselves to powder against the inexorable barrier, trying to reach the light. Aside from the little lives destroyed, the tiny creatures remind me too much of human beings, always trying to reach what they consider light—it's not the same for everyone—and often encountering an invisible wall against which they bruise themselves.

July is a middle-of-the-road month somehow; it does not possess the astonishments of May or the fresh gaiety of June; nor does it, like August, slide silently into cooling nights after burning days. July seems to stand still; dust is on the heavy foliage and fresh-cut hay dries in the sun.

Yet, it brings fireworks and vacations, lazy days at sea and shore or mountaintop; driving madly over congested roads to somewhere else, or standing over an outdoor grill in one's own backyard.

In this month, one expects thunderstorms; there is also increased noise when more people take to the highways; and, of course, here there's heat and its despised sister, humidity, while across the Equator folks go skiing. But in between, you find the brilliant sun, the stars pacing across a black marble sky, or the moon rising purest gold. Now the birds appear only in the cool of early morning, or at sundown, to utter their lyrical comments. Some roses continue to bloom in July and the annuals burst into color in garden beds and borders.

In every season there are days of glory. But they don't have to follow a seasonal pattern. I think, for instance, of a winter wedding, on the morning of an early February blizzard, when a young woman whom I know very well was quietly married. Her only attendants were her two children —girls—and the bridegroom's four—three girls, one boy. The girls, as befitted the season wore red and white for the coming Valentine's Day; the boy, thirteen, acted as best man, grave, conscious of his responsibility, as he handed his father the ring. Everyone had luncheon at a place the children had selected, and later when the bride and groom went away for a weekend wedding journey, they found in their hotel room flowers and a card reading, "With love from your six children."

That was June in February.

Life won't be all starlight and roses with six children to look after, understand, and guide, and while things may be "cheaper by the dozen"—which nowadays, I doubt—they certainly won't all come easily. When you stop to think of it, with one roof sheltering eight people of varying needs—beyond the common ones for food, shelter, education, and clothing—a smooth, quiet way of easy living would be impossible, even if there were millions to take care of the practical side of things. But do we really want easy living?

Those who say, "My life's been hard," think they do. We all think it sometimes. I do. I often tell myself that, if there is another crisis, I shall simply lie down and pull the covers over my head. But I don't. I can't. Remember the ancient legend of the hero who, every time he was hurled to earth, rose again with many times his previous strength? We can't achieve that, of course, but we can at least, get back on our feet.

So, in recent years, when I've said to myself, "I haven't had an easy life," I've added, "Thank God."

If there were no difficulties, people would grow soft; their spiritual muscles would become useless; there would be no strength to draw upon and then, when big crises came, what would happen to them?

Anything to which you can face up—eventually, if not at once—means growth, whether it's illness, bereavement, anxiety, or fear. Most of us have someone near at hand who will share bad times with us. All of us have Someone, even nearer, to whom we must turn if we are to find, and sustain, courage. Maybe this sounds like an on-the-surface attitude, a platitude, a cliché. It isn't, no matter how often it's been said, in how many different ways. If, in meeting whatever comes, you grow through it, you learn, a very little, to understand other people and their similar or different problems. And even a small amount of comprehension turns you outward, not inward.

All of us—even those who are not acquainted with the Psalms—have asked at one time or another, "What is man that Thou art mindful of him?"

Usually we relate the question to ourselves, for whatever else man is, he is intensely personal. And we extend the question; it is not just, "What am I?" but, "Who am I?"

And sometimes we ask, "Why?"

Many men and women, countless numbers of them throughout recorded history, have ascended to great heights of nobility and sacrifice, for does not the Psalmist continue, "Thou has made him a little lower than the angels." And even average people like ourselves have risen to meet the demanding, important occasion. Most of us, during our lives, achieve the heights but rarely, though we often rise above our ordinary everyday level and say, or do, something which is good, spontaneous, purged of ego, and without selfish motivation. And yet, ten minutes, twenty-four hours, or a week later, we may reject a friend, refuse a kindness, or ruin a reputation.

That's a lot lower than the angels, but the physical man wars with the spiritual and in each of us, I believe, there is a Judas which frequently betrays the spirit within. Like the moth against the window in the night, we are closed away from the light, no matter how deeply we long to reach it.

How I'd love to go to bed just one night in a year—maybe in a lifetime—to look back upon the day just closed and know that not once during it had I betrayed myself—and others.

During this month when the clear evenings are long and bright and the birds come out from the sheltering woods, most people, even those not on holiday, take time for a little relaxation, in the cooling-off dusk or evening. You see them all over, sitting on porches, patios, or terraces. You see them in the parks, and the cities, on the streets and, in crowded districts, on fire escapes. The highways and roads are so blurred with traffic, it almost seems that everyone is going somewhere. I like to sit outside and look at the stars, or stand by the pool—which hasn't much water in it during this season—and try to be quiet, within myself. . . . But there is always, of course, the inevitable imperfection; in July, it's usually mosquitoes.

A year ago last summer, I went on a day's trip with friends, upstate and into Rhode Island. Our first objective was the Gillette Castle, now a state park. William Gillette had been an old friend. I'd known him since I was nine years old, but I had never been in the fantastic house he built in his later years. I knew him best when he lived aboard his houseboat, the *Aunt Polly*. However, going to the Castle wasn't as nostalgic as I had thought it would be. I walked through the rooms, looked at his superb view of the river, and thought of all he was and how fond I had been of him. One Christmas, when I was about eighteen, he sent me a beautiful color print of the Taj Mahal because I had once said to him—and he remembered—that I longed to see that exquisite memorial.

This print has disappeared; whether it was lost in the shuffle of time, or in moving, I don't know. But for years it hung where I could see it. I never have seen the lovely building except in pictures. The most I ever saw of India was an airport, where I once waited an hour or so before taking off again, but for a long time I had the dreaming Taj Mahal on my wall, and it is still in my heart—a memorial to love.

I don't expect to be away this month. I'll be home and I'll have a novel coming out, so I'll be bracing myself for criticism and thinking ahead to another book. I'll work and see friends; I'll walk in the fields, looking for wild flowers and hope that Gussie will bring me something bright and fragrant from her garden. So one day will drift lazily into another, punctuated by occasional exclamation points of lightning. There'll be time to think and evaluate a little from this middle-of-the-year—the little-more-than-halfway mark on the road which began in January—and to consider the views it has afforded, what corners it has turned, what dangers have been averted, what obstacles met along the way. Time also to think ahead to the rest of the annual journey and what it will bring. The answer to that is not written in the signature of a swallow's wing across the sky, or in the July stars, nor does it speak in the little wind which comes, scented with roses, to refresh me.

Do you remember back last February when a predicted doomsday did not materialize? I was amazed to find that many of my otherwise sensible friends were disturbed, even apprehensive, some were terrified. T. S. Eliot has said, "This is the way the world ends/Not with a bang but a whimper," and contemplating the uncertainty of some I know, I began to think, that if it did end, he'd be right.

Ah, but personal doomsdays come to us all, and more than once during our time on earth—in change or sorrow, in loss or fear—and we think our individual world has ended. It hasn't, of course, for we go on just as we were intended to—at least the majority of us do—recovering courage, strength, and hope.

What is man, indeed? He is compounded of a thousand things and is not the same man today that he was yesterday; and he'll be a little different tomorrow. Character builds slowly, but it can be torn down with incredible swiftness. We're conditioned by environment and heredity, by emotions and events and circumstances, but most of all by our own thinking.

Not much time has passed since I sat down at this typewriter—how much more romantic if I wrote with a quill! —interrupted only by three telephone calls and going out of the room to switch off lights and close shutters. . . . I came back and apologized mentally to my gray machine for the way I insult its intricate mechanism when I use it, in my inept fashion. . . . No, not much time has elapsed and yet I am not quite the same woman who came into the study a while ago, nor shall I be exactly the same woman I am now when presently I leave it.

Perhaps we should pray daily, "Grant to me, Lord, that I may heed the promptings of the spirit within me and follow its light, even though I fall back, bruised, in the seeking; and help me to offer to the world, open hands, an open mind, and an open heart."

Have a wonderful July, home or away. Don't expect everything to be satin-smooth—all roads have uneven places—but have fun and gain understanding as you head toward August, remembering a recently ended vacation or looking forward to one.

Happy Independence Day. Happy July.

I, July . . .

From July we have inherited mobile jewels—the memory of evenings during which rockets soar upward and burst into colored stars, before returning to earth; the memory of sparklers and of the faces of children sitting, on a hillside, a lawn, or a beach, watching adults set off the anticipated fireworks with the elaborate set pieces as a grand finale.

In my neighborhood such displays are restricted to clubs, organizations, town festivities—not that people don't cross state lines to get around the prohibition. I no longer go to clubs for these gala evenings, but I can sit upstairs on the sun porch, switch off the lamps and watch bright showers of man-made stars, a little mysterious because of the distance. From this vantage point, I am quite far away from the noise, which I dislike.

My younger daughter never liked noise either. I remember when she was very small, and spending one of many summers on the St. Lawrence, the nearby campers' youngsters had firecrackers—not then forbidden—and even tin cans to increase the noise of the giant ones. They used to start fire-cracking in the dawn's early light, so a good, grown-up friend next door took Ann fishing and she came home that evening, in peace and triumph, with a muskie almost as big as she was.

July's own fireworks can come at any time, and all month she celebrates the Fourth, for in the gardens there is the red of roses, the blue of delphinium, any number of white flowers—and also the little stars of gold.

In July's one holiday, we have the harvest sown by brave, sacrificial, dedicated men, the patriots to whom freedom, the American dream, was dearer than their physical lives.

May God preserve it and keep it a reality.

So, thank you, July.

AUGUST

♛

WALKING outside the house this month, I note with dismay, and not for the first time, that it should have been repainted last spring. White houses have to have their faces lifted cosmetically more often than houses of other colors; also, the outside shutters, dark green in the traditional New England manner, are fading. But at least there's a new gutter over the door; the old one had a most disconcerting way of hoarding rain water or melted snow and cascading it upon the heads of innocent visitors as they mounted the steps to ring the chimes.

Someone called Gail Hamilton wrote long ago of "the total depravity of inanimate things," and that there is some such manifestation of malice I heartily agree. Why else does a rocking chair reach out and bite one's ankle? Why am I led to put a carbon between two sheets of paper wrong way around, as I did just now? I am always quarrelling with the bread which falls buttered side down, the button which pops off without warning and creeps under the bed, the slippers which walk away and hide in corners—a dozen such instances un-grace every day. Pictures leap off walls or try to leave their frames and, as for mislaying things, I'm not too sure that I always do—sometimes I think they take off on purpose. This is true of most shopping lists I make and of my numerous pairs of glasses. . . .

This year, the flower boxes set upon the gray stones of the terrace are prettier than usual, as are the big white tubs of geraniums and trailing ivy on the kitchen porch. When there's been no rain, I stagger out with an enormous watering can to coax them to last a while longer. But too soon not much color will be left, though perhaps the mint will still be growing near the kitchen door, and the weather into September remain warm enough for iced tea. The most perfect iced-tea maker I know is my sister, Esther. She inherited the gift, as well as the recipe, from our mother. I've never had the patience.

August makes me think of Cape Cod, where the Spartan roses grow by Gladys Taber's door—I have a few, which were gifts, but they cannot measure up to hers—and the petunias, in the dusk, release a heavenly fragrance. I am writing this so early in the month that I'm not yet sure whether I'll be there this year or not. Even if I am unfortunate and must remain at home or, on some unforeseen emergency, go elsewhere, I can, as always, recapture the look of sand and water, the smell of sun and bayberry, the faces of friends, the trips to the village, the little outings, and the walks with Gladys' Irish on the narrow curving beach. At least I walk; she runs.

August brings back older memories of the St. Lawrence, flowing in blue or gray silence, in calm or storm between us and Canada. I remember sitting on the porch of the camp where I stayed so often with friends, and watching sudden stabbing lightning set a barn afire across the river.

And sometimes it rained on one shore of the river and not on the other. I remember, too, how cold to the swimmer that water was, and I daresay still is.

The camp's gone now, the friends scattered, the land-and-water-scape changed by the seaway, but I'm sure the river itself is the same.

I'd like to go back there and also to the Adirondacks, lifting blunt or pointed peaks into the sky, and, in the sunset hour, miraculously tinted with mauve and blue. I think often of the shifting shadows, the eternal green, the bare rocks; and of the spreading flame which is called autumn. I've seen that country in winter, too, shrouded in snow.

August brings back the many summers at Hilo, my parents' place on Shelter Island—the high hill back of the house, the salt meadows, the beach, and the little bay. I think of swimming from our dock and of sliding, in my more adventurous days, down a long chute into the water. I remember sailing or canoeing with my sister . . . walking, dreaming . . . and the friends who came to visit us.

That was a time of childhood and of growing up, of the careless acceptance of beauty, security, and love; of selfishness and laughter; of discipline and willfulness; and of the little heartbreaks of adolescence which seemed so tragically important.

There were fishing trips on the big old boat and so many picnics, and on days when it rained, I'd lie on my own small four-poster under an airy ball-fringed canopy, reading, eating August apples and the kind of peppermint creams which are no longer made, and drinking, now and then from a glass of cold water, to sharpen the taste.

My sister, although she is much younger than I, remembers the Hilo days too, and shared memories are very sweet.

The seasons and the years are like the Chinese boxes which are contained one within the other; every month, every year is part of the past, and of the future; there is always loveliness to remember, and to look forward to, which is as it should be.

Beauty, we are told, is in the eye of the beholder, but it is also in the heart and spirit. During the winter before last, an artist came here to paint outdoor scenes, which included the house. We'd had a great deal of snow and I was horrified to see him arrive without rubbers. The white stuff, wet and heavy, was inches deep and heaped high on the terrace. He came twice and made three water colors, two of which were given me later by the magazine for which they were painted. I was enchanted, for I'd seen them when he finished, and in the fluency, delicacy, and grace of these winter-pale paintings, he had managed to communicate the atmosphere of the place I call Fable Farm.

One painting had the loveliest sky, with a wash of mauve across it and as I looked at it, he said, "I saw it that way."

I hadn't, not really. I am not an artist and the overtones and undertones he'd seen were not visible to my outward eye, but I know they were there.

Not even the beauty we recognize is entirely visible to our physical sight, I suppose, and it is therefore imperative that we look with an inward vision, not only upon the natural beauty all around us, but at people and even events. This, too, is an art; it is the art of living, of searching, of understanding—or trying to understand—and the most important creative expression which we, while on earth, shall ever know.

I have met people, in all walks and situations of life, who have learned, through the years, to live gracefully. Seemingly, they are never bored or indifferent. They have a certain gaiety of spirit and a visible warmth of personality. They're interested in everything that happens to everyone within their reach. This is not curiosity or vicarious living; it is an extension of themselves, a wish to share, a desire to grow into knowledge.

Some of these people had material wealth, some had none at all, and the majority were everyday strugglers like most of us. This art of living has nothing whatsoever to do with what you have, but with what you are inwardly, and how you grow, and what you become.

Thinking of these artists in living I realize that not one of them had—or has—narrow interests. Oh, all had special interests, of course—we all have—but they never confined themselves to these. Yours were just as important and they seemed always to be asking of all they met, "What do you do? What do you like? Tell me about yourself . . ." in order to know something about someone which they could catalogue, not to repeat later, but that they themselves might learn.

There is actually no one who hasn't something to teach us—however different he may be from us, however incompatible. Perhaps it's from those who aren't compatible that we can learn the most if we make the effort.

Usually, when we speak of a person who has made an art of living, we think of what is called culture—book knowledge, identification with any of the arts, even things like how to order a meal, or value an antique. I once had a friend who rarely opened a book. She was too occupied with a big demanding family which had to be fed, clothed, and educated—all as well as possible on a small income. She wouldn't have known a Picasso from a Monet, and music to her was only a cheerful sound. She loved the flowers in her hand-tended garden and the birds in her trees, but her knowledge of them was not technical. Her main interest lay in life, in living it and giving to it. She was not a woman who wished only to take. Loving life as she did and the people—all sorts of people—who shared it with her, she was an artist in perception, and in her personal expression of the spirit within her.

Early last winter, I had a letter from a reader in which she quoted a sentence I'd never come across before: "I love you, not only for what you are, but for what I am when I am with you." I couldn't find it in my Oxford Book of Quotations; perhaps I could have in Bartlett. But I'd lent my Bartlett to someone and it had not been returned; it just went the way of most borrowed books. Therefore, I could not, when I first quoted it in a magazine article, give the source or credit the—to me—unknown author, for which I apologized. I have since learned that the words are those of Mary Carolyn Davies, and they are words upon which to meditate. I've been doing just that, on and off, since the letter came to me, and it's true that the people who somehow bring out that which is best in us are those whom we gratefully love. We are better than we think we are when we are with them. What this gift is, I do not know. Perhaps it is spiritual understanding.

There are people in whose company we feel gayer, wittier, more intelligent than usual, and those in whose presence we seem to become more understanding ourselves because they seem silently to require from us the best we have to give.

I am certain that the people who elicit this sort of reaching upward and outward from those they meet do not know it. They are unconscious of their gift. Like the mint by my kitchen door, they grow in the sometimes stony earth of human relationships, asking no more than the nourishment of the divine spirit, falling like quiet rain upon the hard and hostile ground.

When we are with them, we really feel better, in every sense of the word. It is not a question of putting one's best foot forward to interest or to impress. The best foot is forward.

"Contrariwise" as Tweedledee said (and that's how Mr. Carroll spells it) there are those who appear to bring out the worst in us—the criticism, the irritation, the sharpness.

I often pray, "Lord, let no one be the worse for knowing me." I've never dared add, "But, rather, better," because I've no confidence in my own ability to uplift. Besides it has a rather egotistical connotation. More importantly, I don't believe we are supposed to receive this faculty as a gift but to build it, by effort within ourselves as we must fashion the other qualities for which we find ourselves praying—courage, strength, and patience, for instance.

Fortunately for me, I've known a great many people who, with no awareness of it, demanded the best that I could give. So that in numberless ways I like myself better when I am with them.

A very few times in my long professional life, I've come downstairs to the study in the morning to sit down and reread what I'd written the day before and feel that it was —while not very good—at least better than I really know how to write. Comparable to this feeling of achievement, which you cannot believe has been brought about by yourself, alone, is the rising to a higher level of consciousness through the presence of another person—rather like a flower compelled to turn its face to the sun.

When the letter from which I quoted came to me, I realized how much I have owed to the goodness of others which, however briefly, has brought out in me that which is also good. Such people can be old friends, known over many years, or strangers briefly encountered and perhaps never to be met again. It doesn't matter. I suppose the lesson here is to recognize and respond to this quality which demands our best.

Sometimes I feel like the youngster who skims through his daily lesson, hoping merely to pass. Many times I look back upon a day—such as this one in August—during which I have been happy in the sun or shade, or walked upon the sand and heard the gulls crying, or just put some roses in a bowl, or talked with old friends, and I think as I go to bed: I didn't take enough from today; I didn't put enough into it. And then I am saddened because this day will never come again except in memory.

How we hurry through our days and our seasons—appreciative often, but still hurrying. We never seem to be able to stop long enough to savor the full essence of the hours. I do not mean that we must stop physically—except for the quiet minutes I've recommended and always try to find—or lie back and neglect what we should be doing in order to contemplate the universe about us. It would be good, of course, if we could extend our quiet time to hours rather than minutes, but almost everyone's days are full, not only of things to be contemplated but of things which must be done. What I really mean is that we should stop hurrying within ourselves.

The bud unfolds slowly; that is its nature; and perhaps the rose knows that it blooms for a short time only.

I just took my hands from the typewriter. Having changed a ribbon for the first time in my life—the ribbon of my new typewriter can be changed easily, even by me—I should go wash up, but I haven't yet. I've been sitting a moment and looking about the room, which was quiet as there was no clatter of keys. A car went by, and a bird spoke its piece, and a dog barked across the street. Despite the awning over the window in back of me, the sun pours in the lower half of the window, and soon it will be westering and shine through the windows to my left. The bright and dark bindings of many books make a pattern. Across from the desk there's an old chair which belonged to my mother. The springs are broken and usually anyone who sits in it jumps up with surprised outcry. I like it; it seems to fit me. Now, there's a spatter of sunlight on that faded upholstery and the milk glass on the mantelpiece is as white as gardenias. This room has been, for the past eleven years, a big part of my life, but I don't think I ever looked at it before as I did just now—like an artist. . . . I'm going to make room in my time-budget for looking at things that way, if only for a moment.

We all know about budgets, the struggle with them; the apportioning of material means, and of time. The bank account reflects how we've managed the one, and the engagement calendar how we hope to manage the other. There's still another budget, however; that of the emotions. In that department we should all try to spend less upon the destructive emotions—anger, fear, annoyance, and impatience—and more on loving and giving, trusting, hoping, and understanding. If we can accomplish this, even in a small way, the accounts will balance in the end and we will have spent with wisdom.

This is the month during which summer fulfills herself, reaping the harvest gifts of other months before she turns her bright face toward autumn, without regret. The year, unlike some of the people who live it, always grows old gracefully and in a particular beauty.

I do not know in what month you will be reading what

I, in August, have written. But I wonder what you are doing, right now. Are you walking on a beach or climbing a hill? Are you sea- or mountain-bound, or staying home to wander in the blue dusk and watch the stars? Are you looking at things new to you, from the windows of a car, a train, a plane? Are you perhaps at the Fair in Seattle, or in a backyard having a cookout with friends?

Wherever you are, whatever you are doing, or planning, happy arrival and departure, happy August.

I, August . . .

The legacy of August is the harvest of the months past and the preparing for the physical harvest to come. The corn is high and the grains and grasses. My fields, to be sure, were cut over in July, but they've sprung up again under the sun and rain.

August gives the birds a little free time, for the building of nests is over. They've taught the young to strip the mulberries from my trees and, in most cases, how to fly. Some of the birds have two families of babies during a summer. I suppose they don't want to sit around and engage in idle musical conversation until autumn's really here.

The month has brought, as did the last, birthdays of people dear to me and I'm always so glad that they were born into a world in which, at the same time, I live.

Golden grain and golden kernel and the zinnias in every color standing straight and tall and the spilled deep sunshine of the marigold. There are August jewels to treasure.

I haven't, as yet, lived much of the month, but whatever it brings, whether I stay here or go elsewhere, I'm grateful for it.

So, thank you, August.

SEPTEMBER

I'M CHEATING a little, for it is still "last month." If I am to go away—and I'm still not sure—there's work to be done first. I don't know anything about this September except what I anticipate or surmise.

A long time ago, I looked in the Farmer's Almanac to see what it said about weather for this Labor Day. It promised, "fine." I hope so, for the sake of those who go away then or who must return right afterwards. . . . Well, happy Labor Day and do be careful.

I don't know when school begins this year. It's been a long time since I've had children in school and my grandchildren haven't, as yet, complained to me that soon they'd be back in what they think of as slavery, though they really enjoy it. If, however, the new term starts right after the third, people may have come home before to get the small fry ready.

How many of them have outgrown shoes and clothes?

Even in August, there's a suggestion of autumn in the

air, a faint, sweet, chill—something reminiscent of melting ice cream, yet curiously, rather like April, also.

I don't like the word "fall." I prefer to say "autumn." It's prettier to begin with, and "fall" suggests decline, the blowing leaf, the downward trail.

I never think of this approaching season as descending, but rather as rising in triumphant beauty to heights of courageous flame. In September, the leaves begin to be bright-hued and Nature, preparing the bed which will, later, be covered and softened by her white down quilts, speaks to the earth of slumber. But there's a reaching out past sleep to reawakening, past the winter to the spring. Man, far from gloomily contemplating the so-called "melancholy season" must, in his inner self, know how marvelous the plan and purpose, wrought of promise and of hope.

No season is truly melancholy. I have friends who dread the early darkness of winter days, who suffer when there is no sun. I am fortunate in that weather has never affected me. Naturally, I prefer that it be good rather than bad—it's more attractive, and also easier to get around in—but my temperament's temperature does not rise and fall with thermometers or barometers.

There is beauty in the bare as in the leafy bough. This month's special loveliness is in the reddening vine, the colorful foliage, the bittersweet berry. Yet it's not to be measured solely by the eye. Surely, the true measure of the spiritual man lies in his instinctive knowledge of the unknown, his ability to see the invisible and touch the intangible and to hear sounds not conditioned by the acuteness of the ear.

To achieve this awareness is a wonderful thing and the smallest success is a widening of spiritual horizons, a reaching toward a goal never wholly to be realized in a lifetime, for as Robert Browning said:

> *"Ah, but a man's reach should exceed his grasp,*
> *Or what's a heaven for?"*

The limitless love of God is not bound by any horizon; it is as close as hands or feet and as necessary as breathing. We can repay this bounty, this immeasurable inner strength, only in the flawed coin of human love for Him and our fellow man.

A while back, a close friend asked me, "Why don't you write about doorstops?" We had been looking at one of hers, which was a cannon ball retrieved by an ancestor from a battlefield. I'd hate to fall over that one.

I have some doorstops, too. Years ago, I was given two, in beautiful, deep green glass. One had something blown into it, rather like a lily. That one I gave away. The other, which is round, heavy, and twinkly, with blown stars inside, I kept. Once, while on the Cape, I went into a shop which specializes in Sandwich glass—I'd never known if my doorstop was Sandwich or Bristol—and spoke to the owner, an expert. I told her that I had this delightful object, rather like a paperweight, only bigger and added that I used it as a doorstop. Then I asked, "What would it have been made for originally?"

She regarded me with the faintly pitying concern of the informed for the ignorant and replied briefly: "Doorstop."

At another door, there's the handmade wooden last for a square-toed shoe; it was found in the barn of the house I had before this one. As a doorstop, it isn't too efficient, not being heavy, but it's a conversation piece and if you stub your toe on it—well, that's appropriate.

For a long time, my bedroom door was held open by a huge china bank. It was a pig with a pink china ribbon about its neck and its name was Rosy. That's gone now, so if there's a wind and the door slams, I put in its place anything that's handy. I hate banging doors and shutters with a fierce hatred. My door to the upstairs sun porch has a magazine rack against it, for windows are open there all summer. The rack is full of old magazines—quite erudite—which no one seems to want.

In my study, I have a doorstop which my son-in-law made for me last Christmas. This is a cat cast in brass, but the texture is rough, and it has a furry look. The back is hollow and red marble eyes have been set in. When first I received it, I put it on the hearth for all to admire, and the eyes would fall out, without warning, and roll over the hearthstone. Now they are steady and firm and if I get up from this chair and take two steps, there's my cat, keeping open the door into the little hall. That's what doorstops are for.

How do we keep doors open, figuratively, and with what do we also lock them? The answer to that last question is keys, bolts, and sometimes chains.

When the doors to the rooms of the heart and spirit are locked, there are all sorts of devices which will keep them closed. Fear is one, and shyness another, the wish never to betray one's self to other people. There are rusty keys which all of us know about—indifference, prejudice, unkindness, and what we call intolerance. There is one very heavy bolt, which I think of as the inability to love and to trust. People who live in such securely locked rooms—where little air, less sun, and no warmth whatever are allowed to enter, in the heart's winter, or the spirit's summer breeze—are unhappy people.

What do we use for doorstops if we wish to keep the doors open? In most material houses, doors are locked at night, which is purely sensible, but the spiritual door can always be kept open. It takes a while to learn to fashion the doorstops; you have to do it yourself. There are no blueprints or directions. If I could have a mythical factory and turn out spiritual doorstops I'd make them from love—not always the easiest material to come by—and from trust. I'd carve them from interest in other people, and in the shape of a listening ear, or an open hand. And I'd make them from the stuff of quietude and, blow into them the wonderful forms which are prayers.

All these, and many more, can keep your doors open for you and for those who desire to cross the inner threshold of your life.

I think of all this now when, between hall and living room, I look down to admire my Sandwich—or is it Bristol?—glass, or contemplate the wooden shoe last or the magazine rack, or, passing by, stoop to pat my doorstop cat upon the head.

Lock the doors of the frame or stone house against unlawful intrusion, or storm, or night, but open them to friend or stranger. And never lock the doors of the heart and the spirit.

Now is the time of harvest in the field; but it is always harvest, for us. Year 'round there is living truth in the old words: "Whatsoever a man soweth, that shall he also reap."

That does not mean, I'm sure, the physical field crops, for, as even amateur farmers know, you can till and sow and the reaping can be frustrated or erased by insects or weather. But that which we sow in word or deed, emotionally or spiritually, we always reap, for good or evil, or in between.

Sometimes bread cast upon the water does not return to fulfill the promise: and if it returns, rarely does it come back to us as cake.

I don't know whether or not you are upset by small crop failures—or the vanishing of the cast bread. The failures are usually irritations and annoyances, and I'm often upset by them and, therefore, ashamed.

Not long since I suffered a crushing blow, and coming as it did after a succession of others, involving other people, I was doubly disturbed. I think that, by now, I can endure almost anything which relates only to myself, but unfortunately almost every ax which falls on us falls as well on people we love.

Well, last spring, a few days after the ax had fallen, I returned from church to find the domestic peace disturbed.

For months, I'd had a plant, a pink and green coleus, given to me in its beginning. It grew and grew and became so heavy that the long drooping branches touched the little table upon which the plant stood; they broke and died. So my good friend, Agnes, devised a plan. She took a little chopping block and upon it set a large glass container, into which she put the plant. It sat only halfway down in the container, grew and flourished and stood so tall the branches didn't reach the table.

But on that particular Sunday—with no one in the house—I came in to find everything overturned, perhaps by a mischievous breeze through an open window. There was damp earth and dozens of pieces of broken glass all over the table, the floor, and a nearby chair.

I cleaned up. I took plant and table into the kitchen, washed off the table and the sheet of glass over the table-top painting my daughter had made of the old house. I put the plant, one heavy branch gone, into a kitchen bowl and went back to sweep up glass and earth. I set the plant in its bowl on a wooden footstool, hoping the branches would clear it; replaced the table. And as I did so, I went about muttering aloud, "This is the last straw."

It came to me, then, through some trick of the subconscious, that you can't make bricks without straw—which didn't, at the moment seem to make sense.

After a while, sitting in the twilight, I began to think that there is no last straw. It's as if you said—and I've said it, too— "I'm at the end of my rope," and then found that you weren't. That rope, like the one used in the Indian fakir trick, keeps spiraling upward; you learn to tie a knot in it and go on climbing.

Using the innumerable last straws encountered in a lifetime, you can, with the proper added ingredients, learn to make bricks. You can, of course, build anything with them. The warning here is: do not build a prison in which to hide yourself; do not build a wall which shuts you in, and keeps everyone else out. Build, instead, a brick path which leads somewhere; fashion a sanctuary to which you can retreat for a while in times of stress; make an altar upon which you may lay your sacrifices; a home for your indomitable spirit.

Most of all, build character. . . .

Character isn't built through ease, success, a million dollars, a carefree life. Few people are so spiritually secure that they can build through prosperity and happiness, for these, when they come, are often taken for granted. Out of pain, sorrow, and adversity are fashioned the bricks which can be used to erect an enduring edifice.

So, if you think the straw in your hand is the last straw,

look for other ingredients and build something of value. For this is the real and everlasting harvest—what you have built from whatever has befallen you.

These are hard lessons to learn, but if there is anything absolutely true—and inherent in the truth which is God—it is that we are here to build, however painfully.

All harvests are wonderful, whether from the fields which had to be harrowed and planted, which had to receive sun and rain, or a harvest from those other fields which must be also tended—perhaps a small seed of kindness which came to flower long after it had been sown in the heart of child or friend—or, most wonderful of all, the harvest of growing character which has weathered all storms.

As I write, I find myself laughing a little because we speak so often of weathering storms and forget what most things look like after weathering. Cape Cod houses are silvery and beautiful, but sometimes, when I look at myself in a mirror after I have weathered a storm, I decide that well-weathered human driftwood is far less attractive. . . .

Well, happy harvest and may all your last straws be used for bricks; may all you planted that was good and true and loving grow for you into glory. And if the crop has had to be sown in what seemed unfriendly soil, may it still flower magnificently under God's fruitful plan and purpose.

Happy September, happy path into autumn, and keep the doors of your mind and heart wide open.

I, September . . .

September is duty bound to bring us a great, golden, Harvest Moon—full, I see by the almanac, on the thirteenth. And though the wild ducks no longer return to my pond—there has been building too nearby and there is an inquisitive dog in the neighborhood—they'll come back to others. And the birds will be gathering to talk about their transportation south.

One bold, bright leaf may turn early, and others will follow as they please; a few may decide to fall and rustle on the terrace; winds will rise and people start to worry about hurricanes. I remember those in past Septembers and one on the very last day of August.

September will bring mellow days and cool nights and to me the remembering of more birthdays and anniversaries—my parents', and that of my older son, and his wife, Janet.

What else the month will have brought me, personally, as it ends, I do not know. If I get to the Cape, I'll have new memories of Gladys and the Irish, of the quiet spacious house, the beach below, the sun all around, the Spartans still blooming, and, usually, the strange odor of salty fog creeping in gray and quiet as a cat.

I hope, if I do get there, I'll bring home some bayberries. I have bowls filled with those of other years and a tall old vase (with a piece now gone from the lip) which was a wedding gift to my grandaunt at the time of her second marriage (she died in 1937 at well over ninety). But the Chinese wall vases at the foot of the enclosed stairway are bereft of bayberries. One day last spring, as I started upstairs, the gray pearls showered all over me. I do not know if they were just tired and, so, loosened their hold upon the black branches, or if the vibration of my footfall startled them from a dream of the place where they grew, free and lovely and wild.

If ever you have tried to sweep up bayberries, you will know I didn't go upstairs for quite a while, for many of them had lodged between the floorboards of the tiny hall.

So perhaps this September will have brought me new branches. I'm certain that, if I am home, Gussie will bring flowers from her garden, as will my friend Alma. Perhaps the few little annuals I have now will stay in bloom late this year. I love September flowers, in field or garden. Spring is spendthrift, summer is lavish, but September has unexpected gifts to offer: her special legacy of jewels is in berries, orange and garnet, ruby and indigo, or black as jet, scarlet as sunset.

The harvest September brings to us was sown in other months and she, in turn, while she remains here, will do her own sowing. Next spring we'll see what she has planned for us.

So, thank you, September.

OCTOBER

Best wishes from me to you on my birthday; many delightful returns of October first. I suppose I should wish you that and then forget all about it. Most of the people I know, both men and women, who are around my age, or even considerably younger, announce dismally, "I want to forget birthdays," and sometimes they admonish me, "Be sure to forget mine." I'm certain they don't mean that; they'd be hurt if I did. And as for my birthdays, I like to remember every one of them.

Not all were gay, not all were free from worry—far from it. As a young woman I suffered from a disease called "Round Figuritis," which had nothing to do with weight. When I was twenty, I believed myself ancient; when thirty came around, I shuddered; as for forty, the less said about that, the better. When I was fifty, my publishers gave me a wonderful birthday party and I began to realize that I couldn't do anything about the years and the way they added up, so I was cured. Sixty was rather dignified, I thought. If I live to be seventy—which means one more year—I think I'll take up a hobby. I never have; I haven't had time. What will it be? And do you suppose my publishers will give me another party? After all, once every twenty years shouldn't too much crowd their social calendar!

I remember a year ago this past spring which, here, at any rate, was terrible—all wind and rain and cold—and how confused I felt about summer. Dates always throw me, as if they were a form of judo. I kept thinking: But when am I going to Long Island to be with my sister? And: Before I go to Cape Cod, I have to go to Colorado. And: How will things fit in? But they have a way of working out.

Sometimes Nature amuses herself by tampering with the taps marked "hot," "cold," "wet," "dry." I don't know whether it's because she has a pixie sense of humor and likes to see the female of the species going somewhere in a silk frock one day and digging out the fur coat the next, or whether she just gets bored, as we all do, and doesn't want sameness. Perhaps she takes pleasure in doing the unexpected thing. That's why we call her Mother Nature, no doubt. I know that for the past two winters she had spells of opening the tap marked "Snow," and more recently that marked, "rain," to say nothing of the one that says "wind," until I began to think that everything had fallen which could fall, except the sky.

Oh, but October is a special month and rarely fails us here, although in some years the autumn foliage is brighter than in others. Once I was in Williamstown, Massachusetts, on my birthday, to spend a quiet week with a friend, do some driving about, and then meet other friends and a couple of my children in Vermont. I woke on my birthday, October first, to two events: a telegram from a friend announcing the birth of his daughter, Lucinda—and to the fact that unusual weather prevailed. It was snowing like mad. Hence the drive we'd planned up the mountain had to be postponed. But the sun was warm and within a day or so we were on our way. The road had been cleared, there were banks of snow on either side, but growing up through them were flowers, goldenrod and wild purple asters, and all about us trees flamed above the white.

October flowers are even better than those of September. Now and then there's a defiant, glowing rose, and I've seen the late annuals still in bloom after some of their leaves were black with frost. For frost in Connecticut can come in September.

This is a special month for me, not because I was born on its first day, nor because I have numerous friends who are October's children, but because it usually holds all the warmth of summer and the crystal clarity of autumn.

Once I was on Cape Cod during October, with Gladys and Eleanor—we drove up on Columbus Day—and the weather was like a golden bell; the days so warm you needed no more than a sweater over your frock, the nights cold enough to warrant heat in the house. We went fishing, too, in a canoe, and caught some wonderful winter flounder. I remember a big one, more than ample for us, which I, for some strange reason named Clarence; I remember walking on Nauset Beach and watching the waves come in from Spain. It so happened that I was having a bad time and what my friends and the Cape itself did for me is beyond words. . . . I remember, too, the October moon—that's the Hunter's Moon, isn't it?—rising orange-gold over the water and cooling off to silver.

Some time ago, I wrote about the necessity of sweeping out the dusty attics of our minds and emotions and of the many things we could, with profit, toss away, while opening all the doors and windows and permitting the sun and air to come in, cleansing and bracing. Shortly afterward, a friend, who has lived a little longer than I, wrote to remind me that you can also collect the right kind of memories, the kind you should keep. She said she always advised her young friends to do just that.

So now, looking back, I review my own collection. I remember just before a birthday—I was nine or ten, I think—my father took me into a large jewelry store, sat me on a counter, and talked to people he knew there. They showed me fabulous—I mean legendary, which is one connotation of the world—jewels and let me hold them in my small hands. I remember rubies and pearls, diamonds and emeralds, and after I had looked awhile and hung myself with costly baubles, my father announced that now he'd buy me a birthday present.

The opal is my birthstone and I saw, presently, a beautiful glittering string of them; naturally that was what I selected and my poor parent nearly fainted, for these were big stones and expensive.

He bought me, however, a slender gold chain set with three small fire opals and I wore it for a long time. I wonder what became of it? Perhaps I gave it to a little daughter. It doesn't matter. I have it still in my collection of memories.

By the time I visited Australia, many years later, I owned, through the kindness of a dear friend, and as a gift from my mother on the first Christmas after I was married, beautiful opals, including the so-called black. I brought home from Down Under a handful of tiny stones, later set for someone in a cluster ring, and I was given the most beautiful black opal I ever saw. But I have never worn, or looked at, any opal without thinking of my father and mother.

I have collected many things which hang like paintings in my gallery of remembrance—the way my parents' summer place looked in the early morning, the dancing blue water, the apple trees, the fields and marshes and my mother's garden, way down to the left as you stood on the old porch. There are pictures of the first time I set foot on European soil, fifty years ago, and of Puerto Rico—where I lived for a year when I was first married—with the sugar cane tasseled in lavendar and bending with the wind; with the mountains beyond and the yoked oxen plodding down the road. I've memory pictures of the houses in which I've lived—the brownstones on Brooklyn Heights and the apartments there, too; the stucco house near the Narrows and many others—homes of friends as well as my own.

Many of my pictures are of London, a city I dearly love though I never saw it until 1954. There is a special one of St. Paul's Cathedral. . . . There are also pictures of New York as, for many years, I knew it—the hotel where my mother used to take me to lunch; and the place where, after a matinee, she let me have three different kinds of ice cream. I remember the old Waldorf Astoria, and especially Central Park in which I played as a child.

Recently I've acquired a collection of Bermuda memories to hang beside those of Jamaica and the Virgin Islands and other dream-sounding places.

But the memories I hold dearest are those of people I have loved, and still love, and of kindnesses which have come to me: the letter, the spoken word, the telephone call, the visitor out of the past, the expression of pure love on someone's face, the small hand in my own, or the big one over it, the laughter around my parents' dinner table, picnics with my friends and children, lazy days upon the water when everyone's reflection was the very essence of affection.

Sometimes I walk through the house and look at my collection of mugs, which are not just objects of porcelain, glass and ironstone, but reminders of the people who gave them to me.

Then there are the Chinese things, some of which belonged to my grandparents; others were brought to me from China years ago by a friend; still others Chinese friends have given me. The latest addition to my Kwan Yins is a wonderful ivory head, which a friend, now in California, sent me at Christmas. Kwan Yin's expression is tranquility itself. I see her serene and lovely face every day, and remember her even when I've left the room where she abides.

I am grateful to my wise friend for reminding me that to collect happy memories as one walks one's road is to have something which remains forever. Remembering is not, in her understanding—or mine—a nostalgic dwelling in the past. It is furnishing a picture gallery in which one may walk at any time, companioned, however physically alone, in the quiet hours. . . . It is having a jewel box overflowing with beauty, like the great shop my father took me to—pearls and rubies, diamonds and emeralds, and, of course, opals—jeweled harvest of the years, the legacy of living—all colors, all shapes, and sizes, in a thousand different settings—treasures you will never lose. They will not become dimmed or dusty, nor will the settings tarnish. You don't need a safe or a strong box and you need not carry insurance. This is your very own, this collection of paintings and jewels, and they will last your lifetime. . . .

Since I wrote that last sentence I have answered some mail, opened a present—it's another mug—talked to the milkman and made several telephone calls. Now I'm back again and reminded that tomorrow is Saturday.

On Saturdays, if I'm home, I have fixed engagements in the neighboring village: first to have my hair done and then to meet with a group of close friends for lunch. We have a sort of informal club and any of the group who isn't ill or out of town turns up for a sandwich and good talk.

But first I go to the hairdresser with whom I hold long, sometimes philosophical, conversations. For many years Henry has worried—with good reason—over my scanty and whitening locks. Despite that, he succeeds in turning me into a markedly elderly glamour girl for, let's say, about a day and a half. It always bothers me when I must go out to speak midweek, for by then all of Henry's efforts have been ruined, sometimes by wind and rain, always by the hours of sleep from which I rise to find my hair net on the floor and my hair as tangled as a sheepdog's, though there's less of it. I also have an unfortunate habit of running my fingers through it in desperate moments when I can't find something—usually the right word.

Not long ago I was sitting under the plastic bubble of a drier—such a nice one; it turns itself off and you don't have to be muffled up in nets and cotton ear pieces under it—and since I was, of necessity, looking toward the floor, I found myself contemplating legs. . . .

It's astonishing what you can learn from them—the very young legs, still shapeless and usually wearing long socks or a species of leotard; the not as young which, in my district, are apt to be stockingless or socked, as it were, up to ankle or knee; the middle-aged legs, and the old, usually wearing stockings, some of which do not fit neatly.

Looking at the row of legs opposite me, I thought of children going to school or playing in a yard; of people golfing and skiing and swimming; of people going to work, walking to shops, getting into trains; of women climbing stairs or taking countless steps around the kitchen while doing their housework.

Mostly I kept wondering: Where do they carry you, the young legs and the old? Where do mine carry me and, sometimes, what for?

The town where I have my hair coaxed into some semblance of order is the one in which I lived for fifteen years. When I moved, it was to another town, only a quarter of a mile across the line, but I still go back to the first one, for it is, in distance, closer to me than the shopping sections of the one in which I now live. The village in which I bought my first country house, back in 1936, has greatly changed, as have all villages, I suppose. Many of the so-called estates —including my modest old farm—have been cut up into developments. The two main streets where the shops are have expanded. As I walk to the hairdresser, I rarely see anyone I know except those in the shops who have, for so long, been my friends.

The other day I had lunch with two friendly women in a town I've long known and admired. I hadn't been there in some time and my hostess pointed out, with distaste, all the new houses. I kept telling her that it was the same everywhere, but she continued to mourn over what we call progress.

There's no use getting upset over it. People have to live somewhere and there are more people than there used to be. There is overcrowding; there is change; old landmarks vanish, and even some of the churches have built finer edifices and occupy more land. Some of the architects have departed from the traditional, and it takes a while to become accustomed to a church in the contemporary manner, and even more so to those which are (they tell us) symbolic.

It seems to me that, wherever I go, shops and restaurants I've known have changed hands, and little remains of the old, except those few estates to which people cling because they appreciate the spaciousness and comfort of the houses built in earlier days.

It's always been the same. When, in 1936, we ventured into the country, complete with four children and an extremely annoyed cat, I learned that a man who lived not far away from us was bitterly complaining. He had a beautiful house, on many rolling acres, but he was considering moving. He said that the village had become too big, the peaceful country had been invaded, and the whole picture had changed; he had bought his place in 1900.

Life is never static. Whether you live in a city, the suburbs, the semi-suburbs or a rural area, everything's bound to alter. You can't do a thing about it, except, perhaps, fight the town planners and the zoning board, and it's likely that you'll lose out anyway. Taxes go up, but maybe you'll have a little more protection for your tax dollar. When I moved to this rural district eleven years ago, the taxes were very low, but we couldn't have all the conveniences that those who lived in the town did. We still don't (I just heard the electric pump to my well go on), but we have more than we used to—now that the taxes have tripled.

During this month, many people will move from the city to the country. If they are within commuting distance—and most of them want to be—they won't find it less expensive. Of course, the farther out they go, the less costly for acreage and houses, but the more inconvenient—fewer trains, or a much longer drive for the head of the house if, as is usually the case, he must work in the city.

On the other hand, a good many people are moving back to cities from the country.

Change is always with us, whether it takes place in a locality, the weather, or within the family itself. Few people remain rooted in one place; and if they physically remain where they've been for years, alteration is all about them.

Life is alternation and so is nature; no two clouds are alike, no two snowflakes; the pattern of storm varies, so does the slant of sunlight.

It takes some time to arrive at the acceptance of change—by which one can mean not just a change of locale, or job, or someone's going away from home. It can also mean attitudes—those of your family as it matures, those of your friends, and your own.

Often, to those of us who are old, change appears terrible, even wrong or threatening. The young, as a rule, accept—even welcome—it, and in their way contribute to it, except those who, insecure within themselves, fight it.

In the over-all picture, however, change is good. It expands the reaches of our minds and presents the challenges without which life might be peaceful but also stagnating.

I used to battle change. When I settled a house—first the old one, then this—I wanted things to remain just where I'd put them. Now I shift them around according to my fancy and the seasons, and I've been giving away a lot. Younger people than I can enjoy the bits and pieces I've acquired through the years. They might as well have them now.

Autumn returns to us, October coasts toward winter, yet it is never the same October. No two leaves are exactly the same color as were last year's. This is not a monotonous one-way-street world. In all our thinking lives change must come, and the sooner we learn to accept and adapt to it, the better for us.

I have accepted changes in the last decade which, had you asked me twenty years ago, I would have said I'd never accept.

But we can accept anything, mentally, emotionally, and spiritually, if we haven't formed ourselves into a set pattern—it's awfully hard then—and if we have within our hearts and spirits sufficient faith in God's plan and impartial justice.

What we've had is ours—be it love, companionship, easy living, or a house in which we felt at home. When these move away from us, then we will have something else. But we will not have lost what was truly ours; it will forever live, if we let it, not only in our subconscious and conscious memory but in our souls, for it becomes a part of our life-tapestry.

Nothing is lost, as the changes take place, and much would be gained if we could see it so. But we have what I sometimes call the worm's-eye view, so very close to the ground, so limited. The bird's-eye view is what we need as we look back and forward over the great sweep of the past and future.

A wise man once said to me, "Go with the cosmic tide and not against it"; and, recently, another said, "Row with that tide."

Never against it. Rest on your oars now and then . . . and remember . . . and think about your collection of memories.

I've written more about October than most other months, perhaps because it begins my personal new year, and I look ahead to a little more collecting and look back also at the lovely accumulations of the years past.

So, many happy returns of my birthday. Add to your priceless collections in the coming months, and, as you rest on your oars, drift into the gold and scarlet glory of October.

I, October . . .

October has left us with a harvest of multi-colored beauty. To me she has brought the beginning of my seventieth year, the remembrance of work done, and a reminder of still more to do.

In this year, I'll have two more books; during the summer, a novel; and late this autumn, the one you are, I hope, reading now.

It's a good month in which to work, this one, although, looking through the windows at the dazzle of sun on leaves, I'm tempted to put the typewriter to bed and go outdoors. The leaves have begun to fall and that's a reminder that, very soon, the branches will be bare and black against a winter sky.

But winter's an even better time to work. There's not quite so much inducement to rush out and play, unless you ski or skate, and I don't.

When I was born, I think October said, that Sunday, "Here is a child who will work for the greater part of her life, and yet who is, I'm afraid, integrally lazy. She'll have that—among other things—to conquer."

I haven't, entirely. There are so many times when I'd rather be somewhere else than in this study. . . .

Meanwhile, I remember October in Hawaii and Down Under. I remember October on the Cape and at Hilo Farm. I remember so many Octobers . . . and I am grateful for them all.

So, thank you, October.

NOVEMBER

It appears that everything possible has been said about Thanksgiving by thousands of people down through the years since the first Thanksgiving was celebrated. There are few new ways in which to state old truths. I've tried and failed.

This year, Thanksgiving came so swiftly. I haven't as yet really said "good-bye for a while" to October. November must have turned the corner when I wasn't looking; but then, summer did, too.

Here and there in someone's garden a rose or an aster has ignored the calendar; some zinnias, too—but not many, for there's been frost.

There is nothing to look at through the study windows—no flowering branch, no wild flowers scattered in the tall grass. No, that's not true; there are the pines eternally green, the notched leaves of the holly with the berries turning red, the dark outlines of deciduous trees etched against a gray sky, which looks very much as if it were thinking about snow.

This year I think I'll bring remembered summer into the house for Thanksgiving. I do have green pine boughs about and dried arrangements of flowers; yellow, jade, and striped gourds; berries and grain; but I can still have summer, by recalling rose time.

The terrace flower boxes and the tubs of geraniums have been taken away and now and then an oak leaf rattles across the brick path or blows over the back porch. Tenacious things, oak leaves, most of them still clinging stubbornly to the trees.

Here, November can be, after its own fashion, as pleasant as early spring. And I have waked up mornings in March and even in April and seen a glaze of ice glittering over the water in the birdbath. But both spring and the November sun can be hot and heartening and the ice gone between one moment and the next.

Warm days, cold nights—I often speak of these because I enjoy them. They always make me think of Palm Springs—so hot in the daytime, but as soon as the sun slides behind the mountains you run for a sweater, and you always need blankets over you at night.

I'd like to go back some year, just as I wish that some Thanksgiving would find me on Cape Cod.

By November, the seasonal chores should be about done. This house, for example, gets turned back to winter, sometime after Labor Day. Little by little summer things are put away and winter woolies come out of their camphor-scented hiding. Before November, if we are forehanded, we should be able to sit back and enjoy the autumn. This carefree period rarely comes to me, as there's always something I've forgotten. I remember last year when I went looking for something in the attic—I don't recall what it was now—and it took two telephone calls, several trudgings up and down a ladder—which, incidentally, stuck and wouldn't slide back overhead where it belonged—and the arrival of helpful friends, before the mission was accomplished.

Oh, now, I remember what I was looking for. We had been promised our first snowfall and I was searching, house-wide, for my old comfortable snow boots. In the course of this lost-treasure hunt I discovered the pale blue suede bedroom slippers, which my younger son and his wife had given me a Christmas or two before. They are lamb's-wool lined and reach above my ankles. I'd forgotten them over the summer, when lamb's-wool bedroom slippers are the last thing you think about. So they came flying down the ladder and were gratefully received . . . to go barefoot on these old floors, which are oddly enough not double but single, could be very chilly to the toes!

At the other house where we had big flower and vegetable gardens, the summer was a madhouse of preserving and for weeks the whole place smelled wonderful. It was fragrant with spices and fruit, and when the tomatoes were ready, the kettles blazed with color. When the tiny cucumbers were pickled, or the watermelon rinds, I wouldn't have changed the odors for all the perfume of the Riviera.

But those days have gone, except in my memory collection. There's no vegetable garden here and no one to preside over the canning kitchen. But now and then friends bring me something from their kitchens: Gussie makes wonderful crab-apple jelly—and some years I have apples to give her from my one crab-apple tree. Agnes makes marvelous apple sauce and last spring a friend brought me, on her return from Florida, a big jar of homemade guava butter, which is delicious.

I just went out and checked in the little pantry and was happily amazed at the array: homemade pickles and relishes from Southbury, in this state; figs from a friend in Texas; half a dozen conserves from one who lives not far away; to say nothing of the lovely passion-fruit jelly which a friend made and gave me in Hawaii and which I haven't dared open, I count it so treasurable.

I am not homesick for the old ways of the other place and years because they would have made no sense here; living alone, entertaining simply, there would be no use, or need, for the shining jars, neatly stacked, row upon row, on cellar shelves. The household has shrunk to just me; the children are not here; the days of many guests coming and going have also vanished; and there is, thank heaven, no war emergency which premises stocking your shelves with home-made products. And the supermarkets aren't far away.

I have never had any wish to hoard; my instinct is to give away everything I cannot use and to throw out what suddenly seems to have cluttered up attic and cellar, bureau drawers and desks. Now and then someone asks me sadly and in wonder, "Didn't you save this or that from your childhood?" And not too long ago I was asked if I wouldn't lend my wedding dress to be shown at an antique fashion show. I love the word "antique" in this connection, but I suppose anything worn in 1920 would seem somewhat aged to people who weren't born then.

No, I don't have my wedding dress. All brides are beautiful (at least in someone's eyes), but their wedding dresses aren't always. If you will leaf back over costume books, or perhaps through your own memory, you will realize that the fashions of the 'twenties were a little odd, although now and then, they—whoever *they* are—try to exhume them. I remember my wedding dress—of ivory satin, straight as plumb line and ending barely below my knees. It had a seven-foot train of rosepoint lace sewed on satin and depending from my shoulders. I haven't even kept the photographs. They'd horrify me.

There is extant, however, a picture of me as matron of honor at my sister's wedding. That dress isn't too bad, being a mass of ruffles, but the hat gives me pause. . . .

No, I cannot live in the clutter of the past and I feel freer when, little by little, I unchain myself from possessions. So, I didn't keep my wedding dress or a great many other things. The past remains in the memory, it need not be stored in an attic.

It's also good to go through the attic of the mind, discarding all the anxious unhappy thinking of past months and finding the things for which all year we have been grateful, but which, having once said, "thank you," we have promptly forgotten. This might be a therapeutic exercise for the Thanksgiving season, after we have recovered from the turkey and the fixings.

I think I'll throw the remembrance of viruses and such into the dustbin and make a vow not to put my gratitude into mothballs to be taken out just once a year. I'll keep it around where I can use it every day.

Most of us, in times of stress, or trouble, turn to God, asking for help and strength; and most of us, when good comes, forget to be continuously grateful; oh, we may say thank you, although if we do, it's usually only once. That isn't enough.

Perhaps it isn't enough at Thanksgiving or at any other time to say, "Thank you, God for the answered prayer, and for all you have given me." I believe we have to learn to be grateful also for the prayer which wasn't answered just as we hoped it would be, for the things which have been withheld, and even for the times I've spoken of as last straws, or the grief which has helped us to understand another's.

Someone way back in my family—my grandmother, perhaps, or a grandaunt—used to say, "We'll make do," when someone came unexpectedly to dinner and there wasn't quite enough of whatever had been planned, or when, in sewing, she ran short of some material.

So this Thanksgiving I promise myself to "make do" with what I have about me, remembering all that has been given and knowing that more will be.

Funny, though, how things we once thought so important lose their hold over us during the passing years—things we thought we simply had to have. Perhaps we had them after a while; perhaps we never had them; but if, in the course of living, we moved on to other necessities and forgot those we once thought of as vital, or if we discarded the desire for them, we were "making do."

My mother's garden at Hilo Farm was a big one; it was informal, beautiful, and well tended. In those summers on Long Island she never had to "make do," as far as house flowers were concerned. Nor does my sister in her summer garden now. But occasionally our mother grew a little tired of the lavish and cultivated and sent me, as a youngster, out into the fields to pick wild flowers. I usually resented this because I felt I had other and better things to do. But I'd go with a couple of baskets and come back with daisies or butter-and-eggs, Queen Anne's lace, goldenrod and asters, or the flowers called everlasting, and even with delicate grasses, rosy or mauve or pale gold—there were so many wild flowers, summer-long, in those fields. And from these she would fashion her lovely arrangements. Only she didn't call them that. She just said, "I'll fix the flowers. They won't last, of course, but they're pretty and different."

She taught me how to fix flowers, too, and after I was older I used to "do" all the flowers for the house.

Her early training marked me. When there's nothing in my half-moon garden bed, when Gussie hasn't had time to pick from hers, I "make do" with something just a field away. Even when there is bloom about the house or Gussie brings me pails full of color, I sometimes go out in the fields —usually after a rainfall, for I haven't much sense—and, attempting to avoid poison ivy, look about for something to bring back. I return, dripping wet, with a basket of sturdy or fragile wild things which flourish in field and wood—wild lilies for instance, sprays of blackberry blossoms, the sweet star-of-Bethlehem. I've been known to bring in milk-weed and thistles, for their color.

This Thanksgiving, in addition to being grateful for the memories of spring's bright blaze, for summer's generosity, and for the flame of autumn, I think I'll be grateful for having had, many times in my life, to "make do." Maybe at the moment I didn't like it much; it's rather like having your heart set on silk and finding that you have to have cotton instead, or looking on the menu for steak and settling for hamburger, or wanting an orchestra seat and finding yourself in the balcony—rather far back.

You can "make do" with almost anything. It is not so much a matter of substitution as adjustment. All our lives the majority of us, no matter what our circumstances, find that, in one way or another, best known to ourselves, we must take, and adjust to, the half loaf.

There are some things for which there are no substitutions and you know them as well as I. You either have God or you haven't; you either love or you don't; either you are loved, or you are not.

Someone said to me the other day that, after long searching, he'd finally found a job and added that he didn't like it. You could see him making up his mind never to like it and refusing to "make do" with it and adjust—or if he was "making do," he wasn't doing it gracefully.

I feel that if we can hold fast to our basic necessities for God and love we can "make do," we can adjust and we can manage our physical and material lives. The necessities of physical life are plain enough—food, shelter, work. Adjustments can be made there and often are. I like caviar, for instance, but if I never saw it again (and I don't see it too often), I would certainly not feel starved. A smaller house is easier to cope with than a big one, less property is less care; and a job we do not like, may, in the long run, teach us more than the one we think we'd like so much.

I believe we should be grateful for the ability, with which many of us are born, to adjust and to go forward. I've known a few people in my time who did neither and I've been sorry for them, and a little impatient with them.

I've seen so many others accept and "make do" with surroundings and circumstances far less comfortable than those in which they'd spent a large part of their lives. I've seen them adapt themselves to failure, to personal loneliness, and the fading dream. I've seen them rise above crippling disease and constant pain. The fortitude of the average human being is marvelous beyond expression.

Now in the November weather, with the ears of corn hanging at the door—birds come and eat mine, the red and black and yellow kernels—and with the sense of excitement which we take with us into this season and the one beyond it, let us take time to be grateful for all we've had as well as for what we now hold, and most especially for the knowledge that God lives within each of us, for the certainty that we are loved and love in return, for all the great intangibles. Knowing these, we can surely "make do" no matter what happens.

Everything is proportionate. When you have a great many flowers, you cut and arrange them, you are happy with them, but you do not look at them with astonishment. In November if one remains blooming outside, it is a matter of wonder.

In this season I appreciate my house plants more than I do when there are plants and bushes and flowers outside. They are spring and they are summer—brought into the house. When the snow starts to fall, as soon it will, I can regard the blowing white outside and the growing green within, and be grateful.

Sometime during this month or very early next, I'll be going, I hope, to see Gladys Taber, not on the Cape, but at Stillmeadow, an hour and a half away by car. We will sit by the fire, near the enormous very old hearth, and we'll talk of all that has taken place since last we saw each other. There'll be a little shop talk, too, but not much, although we are both writers; mostly we will talk of times remembered and friends unforgotten, of our children and their children and of places and people. We'll watch a little TV and maybe go out to dinner once if the weather permits; we'll sleep late in the morning and stay up late at night, as friends will. And I'll walk down to the mailbox and bring back the mail in a basket while Holly races around the yard, not being permitted the dangers of the road. The Irish will be glad to see me and will imagine, of course, that she's a lap dog and come bounding up to sit on my knees while I tell Gladys about Bermuda, for she has friends and relatives there.

So I hope the weather holds and I can go before the time of the turkey, or before December storms. . . . If I can't, I'll be sorry, but I'll "make do" through telephone calls and postage stamps.

Now the first flakes, as predicted, are lazily spiraling to the ground; I don't think they'll stay there; this is just a preview. I'll put on the lights and close the shutters and go upstairs and read until it's time for dinner.

Happy Thanksgiving, all year round, to you and to those you love.

I, November . . .

November leaves us her color. Perhaps you don't think she has color to give, but she has. After the bright leaves are gone, a few hardy ones remain, and the color of the oak leaves, a pink-brown, faded and lovely, is something I always welcome. For years, I've been looking for a tweed just like it.

There are jewels in November, too; the scarlet of the elderberries in the woods, for instance.

November has brought us Thanksgiving and a reminder that it isn't, really, just one day in a year, set aside by Presidential Proclamation. It's for every day. Of course turkey every day would be somewhat wearing, but the giving of thanks can be for any time and any hour—and should be.

I am grateful for so much, and each day for something more. Sometimes it's a negative gratitude, for when a day's been very difficult, I'm glad that it ends; but glad, too, that in all probability I'll open my eyes, after sleep, on a new one.

Nowadays it snows here more often in this month than it did in years past. I remember a Thanksgiving snowfall which the weatherman said was the first in forty years. I also remembered forty years before that, being driven through city streets in a sleigh to my grandmother's for dinner.

The old order changeth, but sometimes it returns.

I am grateful for Thanksgivings past, for this one, and for those to come. I am grateful for collected memories and for the tide which takes me toward the source of all living.

The legacy of Thanksgiving is gratitude, the harvest is love.

And I have birthdays to recall in this month, which takes us into the Christmas season; and a wedding anniversary, my own.

So, thank you, November.

DECEMBER

Now I am offering you a thirteenth month, so that I may write of another Christmas. There are, of course, people who for years have advocated thirteen months of twenty-eight days each. They claim everything would then be neat and tidy. . . . But would it really come out right? I just tried to figure it on a scratch pad and it looks odd. It's hard enough for me, despite the old rhyme, to keep track of the present twelve months and how many days each one has.

I like the figure thirteen and my father did, too; neither of us considered it unlucky. Once, when I was about twenty-two, I was to have elective surgery and was permitted to choose the date. I said firmly, "Friday, the thirteenth," and so it was.

I like black cats, and if I don't walk under ladders—well, that's just common sense. I hate spilling salt because it has to be swept up—but sugar is worse, particularly on the kitchen floor.

Anyway, in this personal almanac, there are thirteen months.

So now we move toward another Christmas. I can't tell you about this one in retrospect, not having lived it as yet. There are times when, if I'm very tired, I don't believe I'll make it from one Monday to the next Thursday, let alone one Christmas to another. But if I achieve this one, I believe that the same things will go on here as in other Christmas seasons: the ornaments will be brought out, the house put in its Christmas bib and tucker, and I'll see my children and the friends who always come to me at this time.

For some years now, I've been alone on Christmas mornings, but I hope I'll not live long enough to tire of coming downstairs, looking at the tree, and taking from the fireplace the fat stocking which children and friends have filled to overflowing. It will be of no significance that I shall have trimmed the tree myself some days before Christmas, and will know just what it looks like. On Christmas morning it always seems new and special; it comes as an astonishment and a surprise and after I've looked, I'll go put the coffee on, take my stocking back up to bed and unstuff it. When that's done, I'll come down again, bring the coffee into the living room and enjoy the tree for a while.

In the familiar the unexpected can lie. I've never grown up, I suppose—very few of us do—so the old child retains the sense of excitement and wonder on the Eve and on the Morning.

Now, for another year, under the tree will be the red felt cloth, laid over the old green one—the red one with my name embroidered on it. It came to me last year, wrapped around a beautiful footstool which had been embroidered in a pattern of sea shells and was made for me by the two friends whom I call "my girls." And also from last Christmas, I'll have the earmuffs for doorknobs; there are two of them, one green and one white; one has an angel head and the other sequin berries; and both have bells. They keep the doorknobs warm and gay. I look forward to these and to much older things, for once put away, I'm apt to forget them in the twelve months between.

Last spring I watched a young friend gently trapping and banding birds. We had a long talk about the process concerning which I knew very little; he explained it all to me and showed me the tools he used. I watched him take the birds from the trap and bring them indoors to put into what he called "cells" until they were banded; and I saw with what confidence they lay quietly in his practiced, knowing hands—not that they didn't nip him occasionally. I thought thereafter of the birds released and flying free, some of them to turn up in places where they were not expected and be identified by the bands which would tell the experts where they'd come from and, I suppose, by whom they'd been banded.

In a sense, we too, are banded before we fly out upon our long, instinctive, and sometimes far-flung, journeys from the Hand of our Creator to our ultimate destination.

In a material way, this not-yet-experienced Christmas will—if the past provides any clue—bring me gifts: new mugs, perhaps, doorstops; something Chinese; books and flowers, fruit and delicacies—the imaginative love of friends translated into things which can be made or purchased. But what else?

A deeper understanding, I hope, of the season and a sharper urge to express gratitude to many people, those I know and hundreds I've never met, to the world, and to Him Who made it.

I think of December birthdays of those dear to me, some of them not here to celebrate with me. I have always been a little sorry for children born close to Christmas day because they rarely have as many birthday gifts as those born in other months.

The small scrap of earth upon which this house was built, a long time ago, may have turned hard with frost, or perhaps this December will be mild. I cannot foretell weather. But one day it's bound to be December twenty-fourth and the next the twenty-fifth. If anything's certain, it's the succession of days, weeks, and months, and I know that in December, this part of the country will have turned its face toward winter and the shortest day.

Actually, as we live mainly in psychological time, the longest day, in June, can be brief as a blown kiss and the shortest day—in December—as endless as eternity. Yet, every year, after that December day, each succeeding one is a fraction longer; and following each year's longest day, in June, the days imperceptibly shorten.

But every day the world shrinks. I remember that my first plane flights were made in Hawaii in 1938. I was scared stiff, but I was on a magazine assignment and I had to fly from island to island in order to save time. The next year, going from Hawaii to Australia, with a day or so in Samoa and Fiji and a month's stopover in New Zealand, we crossed the Tasman Sea by boat. It can be rough, and they used to rate each trip from one to ten, the mildest being one, the roughest ten. This one had an eight rating. I was at the Captain's table and, staggering to meals, I always found myself walking uphill, and the calves of my legs perpetually ached. A few years later, in 1954, I flew from New Zealand to Australia in a matter of a few hours, in a plane as steady as a healthy heart.

Thinking back, I am astonished at the mechanical progress during the years of this flying age. I haven't thought much about it until now. I daresay any progress, whether in our outward or spiritual lives, comes almost unnoticed. Suddenly you realize it's there. In the inward life, you are aware that you're less tense, more patient or trusting; but that hasn't really taken place overnight. . . . Only a few have traveled the road to Damascus. The rest of us must live years, and experience a great deal, before progression is felt.

In my lifetime, science, in all its branches, has moved ahead—that didn't happen overnight either. It took many years of thinking and planning; of men's dreams, some not realized during their lifetimes; of hard unremitting work and sacrifice.

Nothing of a progressive nature is really sudden, any more than the stars or moonlight are sudden. Hurricanes and earthquakes aren't either; they take a while to form and move into our physical vision. Now we have devices to chart them and follow their courses, which once we didn't have. So, we are warned; yet storm isn't sudden—not even the tornado.

I don't suppose the earth is revolving more rapidly on its axis than it ever did. But we, ourselves, seem to be in an accelerated perpetual-motion sort of spin in every department of our lives. Now and then it's well to slow down in our planning and personal activities, even in our thinking—slow down and contemplate the turning of the wheel, the stars—very bright in December—the orderly phases of the moon, all of which existed before our so-called progress and which will exist long after us, whether or not we wholly conquer Outer Space.

Sometimes people say to me, "I must be getting old. If such and such a thing had happened to me a few years ago, I would have lost my mind (or maybe they say, "blown my top")

But it isn't getting old, I think, or what the books call mellowing; it is the wearing thin of the barrier between the body and the spirit so that, after a while we come, however dimly, to realize what is important and what is not.

No one I know has been more beset with frustration, anxiety, tension—and all the rest described by various catch words—than I. . . . I still am, at times, but over the years I've learned to understand what is vital and what isn't and not to expend my emotional and nervous energy on something which cannot be helped or corrected. Oh, if it can be remedied, you gird up your loins and try; but if it can't, there's no earthly—or heavenly—use in destroying yourself with worry which is physically as destructive as anything can be.

At my age, it is natural to slow down; a physical sort of protocol they tell me. I don't see it that way exactly. I am fairly courteous to my body and respect its present limitations—and I do forget names and telephone numbers—sometimes, including my own. But the slowing down of which I speak is not so much of the mind or body as of the inner life, a sort of relaxation and long quiet breath, a withdrawal and a steady growing into trust. I think you have to live quite a while before—barring infancy—you truly trust. Prior to that, you dream, you believe, and you hope, but trust is something else again—a hidden, enduring strength upon which to draw.

Now that it's Christmas and you look forward to giving—as you do, I'm sure, all year round—wrap whatever you give with love, seal it with understanding, tie it with integrity, and put upon it the shining symbol of prayer. You know there are things no one can buy—intangible gifts that can be purchased only with coins which do not diminish and cannot be devaluated. The more you spend of these golden coins of the human spirit, the more you have.

From Christmas we go into a new year and now's the time to think about resolutions—if you make them. I don't. There are many things I would like to do in the year which is just around the bend. So I tell myself to plan and then, if I cannot accomplish what I wish, to dismiss it. After all, I shall have had the pleasure of dreaming. No one realizes all his dreams, as I've said before. It's better so. If we had everything, there'd be nothing left to wish for and where would the future lead? In a straight line, perhaps, instead of around corners, but turning corners is half of living.

What can I give to you, friend or stranger, for this Christmas, and to take into the new year? Only the confession of my own blind stumbling around the corners, and a little of what has come to me in the way of light and knowledge—not wisdom, for that I do not possess. In telling you that I, too, have grieved and feared, I can give you the gift of understanding somewhat your sorrow or your doubt.

In this season, unlock the doors of which I have written; put the stops in place, open windows and hearts, eyes and ears; open your hands—for what you give you keep forever.

Now we go steadily under brilliant stars, toward the sound of carol singing, toward the tapered flames of the seven-branched candlesticks, and the days which will usher out the old year and bring in the new. What will come to you and to me this Christmas I do not know; what the new year will bring us I cannot remotely imagine. But whatever it is, having life and trust, we can meet it.

Not long ago my older daughter sent me a composition written by her small daughter. Laura's class had been given certain words to weave into a story which, their teacher told them, was not to be a true one. On the first page of my granddaughter's flight into fancy the reminder, "*not ture,*" was written. Somehow, spelled that way, it looked even more not true.

The story itself I found entertaining, but the last lines of it were as unexpected as anything in published literature and out-Henryed O. Henry.

I quote without Laura's ten-year-old permission:

"So I said I would run ten miles if my mother and father got angry, and they were angry, so I had to run ten miles and I never came back."

With some variation, I feel like Laura's heroine. If you have remained with me through the pages of this little book, and if, sharing with me the thirteen months with which it deals, you have been angry, or bored, or have not found some small gift from me, why then, perhaps I should run ten miles and never come back. . . .

Have a happy Christmas, and God bless you.

I, December . . .

It has been said:
A time to wake and a time to sleep;
A time to sow and a time to reap;
A time to harrow, to cast the seed
Of next year's bread for next year's need.

Golden the harvest, heavy the grain
Sown in silence, nurtured in pain,
Tended by love and guarded by hope,
Beginning in darkness, upward to grope;

Thrusting through earth, emerging in sun
The harvest, the harvest, a full cycle run.